Beyond The Razor's Edge

Beyond The Razor's Edge

♦

Journey of Healing and Hope Beyond Self Injury

*Judy Redheffer and Sarah Brecht
with editorial assistance by Michelle
Matos and Jennifer Marx*

iUniverse, Inc.
New York Lincoln Shanghai

Beyond The Razor's Edge
Journey of Healing and Hope Beyond Self Injury

Copyright © 2005 by Judy Redheffer and Sarah Brecht

All rights reserved. No part of this book may be used or reproduced by any means, graphic, electronic, or mechanical, including photocopying, recording, taping or by any information storage retrieval system without the written permission of the publisher except in the case of brief quotations embodied in critical articles and reviews.

iUniverse books may be ordered through booksellers or by contacting:

iUniverse
2021 Pine Lake Road, Suite 100
Lincoln, NE 68512
www.iuniverse.com
1-800-Authors (1-800-288-4677)

In no way has the SAFE Alternatives® program been involved in the creation of this book, nor does SAFE receive any monetary remuneration from this book or any resulting developments from this work. Names may have been changed to protect the privacy of people cited in this book.

ISBN-13: 978-0-595-36026-0 (pbk)
ISBN-13: 978-0-595-80476-4 (ebk)
ISBN-10: 0-595-36026-2 (pbk)
ISBN-10: 0-595-80476-4 (ebk)

Printed in the United States of America

What is S.A.F.E. Alternatives®?

S.A.F.E. Alternatives® program is a unique healing method for the treatment of the purposeful act of self-harm inflicted upon oneself. It is presently located in suburban Chicago at Linden Oaks at Edwards Hospital. For more information on self-injury, please go to selfinjury.com or call 1-800-DONTCUT.

Acknowledgments

Judy Redheffer thanks the wonderful staff at the S.A.F.E. Alternatives® program, for without them, this book would not be possible. My life and so many others have been changed because of your hard work and patience. I also thank the courageous individuals who wrote down their stories and poured out their souls in order to help and support those whom still suffer. Special thanks to Joni Nowicki, Karen Conterio, and Wendy Lader of the S.A.F.E. Alternatives Program for their kindness and support. I would also like to thank loved ones who supported me through the process these last few years including Mark Redheffer, Jennifer Marx, and Joyce London, Jill White, Colleen Olijnyk and Jamie Pasquale. Thank you all for your love, friendship, and patience! Finally, I would like to thank my niece and nephews, Michael, Tony and Nicole Granato for their constant love, you have been my light through the darkness.

Sarah Brecht would like to thank Wendy Lader and Karen Conterio. Thank you for the S.A.F.E. Alternative Program, where would self injurers be today without it? Thank you Joni Nowicki for all of your help and encouragement with this book, you are one in a million! Thank you to the staff members who have worked in S.A.F.E. for pushing us everyday to get the most out of the program. Thank you to all who have shared your stories in this book, you have given selflessly to help so many others. Thank you to Judy Redheffer, for being my co-author and my friend.

I would like to personally thank my family, for the love, understanding and support they have given to me in my life and with this book. Thank you Mom, Dad, Julie, Chris, Jody, Kevin, and Sean, I love you all. I would also like to thank my friend, Jan Wise, who continues to push me to the best I can be, and who is there for me no matter what. Also, I would like to thank Brian Dewyre and Parmadale for laying the ground work to my recovery and always seeing potential in me. Thank you to Toni Powell and Dr. Richard Chase, your understanding and support is priceless.

Foreword

This book is filled with the stories of courageous people determined to enjoy life free of Self-Injurious behavior. They are living examples of S.A.F.E's acronym, Self Abuse Finally Ends.

We developed the S.A.F.E Alternatives Program almost 20 years ago with the belief that choosing self-injury as a coping strategy will inevitably drain people of their identities, productivity and happiness. Rather than collude with our clients perceived weaknesses, we focus on helping them to embrace their strengths. We believe that no matter what they may have been through in life, identifying and facing their issues is a healthier choice than buffering feelings with self-injurious behaviors.

Our hearts have been touched by so many people who against all odds, worked hard to persevere and commit to allowing themselves to tolerate intensely uncomfortable feelings and challenge ensuing irrational thoughts rather than turn to the temporary quick fix of self-injury.

Judy and Sarah are two such remarkable women who are testaments to the resiliency of the human spirit. Their goal is simple; to empower individuals to make healthier choices by sharing what has worked for others.

Karen Conterio & Wendy Lader

S.A.F.E. Alternatives
1-800-DONTCUT
www.selfinjury.com

A journey of a thousand miles must begin with a single step
—a Chinese proverb

The first time I went to S.A.F.E. I was very ambivalent. I really didn't know how I felt about going because I was told that I was going no matter what. My psychiatrist had heard about S.A.F.E. on our local news channel and he knew that I would benefit from the program. My life was so far out of control no one really knew how to help me. Off to S.A.F.E. I went with very little hope and dreams of getting better.

I will admit, when I went to the program the first time, I wasn't ready to get better. I tested the waters a lot when I was there and I was almost asked to leave. However, I finished the program and I went home. I did well for awhile, but it didn't last because I chose not to use my impulse control logs or the other tools taught by S.A.F.E.. I was still rebelling even a month later.

Several years went by with more and more injuries. My life became more and more out of control, to a point where I didn't even know who I was anymore. I had become my self-injury and my own identity was lost. I knew that I had to go back to S.A.F.E. or I would die. It came down to me wanting to either live or to die because I knew that if I kept on the dangerous path that I was on, I would surely die even if those weren't my intentions.

After corresponding with Wendy, I went back to S.A.F.E.. This time I was ready to face my demons no matter how hard it was going to be. I had to face my deepest and darkest secrets that I had hidden for so long. It wasn't easy but I knew I had to do this for myself if I ever wanted to get better. I finally realized I didn't have to keep punishing myself for all the horrible things that happened to me when I was a little girl. Each and every time I injured, I gave everyone who ever hurt me the power to hurt me all over again. I finally said no more and I chose to get better. However, when I left the program, I had no idea what my life was going to be like. I had no idea that my journey to recovery had just begun. What I thought was complete at S.A.F.E. was only the beginning in my recovery. I was about to embark on even bigger challenges because I was no longer in a "Safe" environment. Rather, I was in the real world with a lot of choices, positive and negative.

I did really well in the beginning, but slowly I fell right on my face. This time I picked myself up and started again with the courage to beat self-injury and the demons that haunted my life. I think I fell more in the first couple of months than I did prior to going to S.A.F.E. the second time around. I got discouraged, but I had my family and friends by my side to cheer me on. Of course I am the one who had to make the decision not to injure or to do anything else reckless.

I soon realized that the friends I once had could no longer be my friends because they weren't healthy. I found myself drifting in unhealthiness when I was around them. I knew it wasn't good for me if I wanted to stay injury free. It was hard walking away, but I wanted to get better more than anything and if I wanted to be healthy then I knew I had to find different friends. I needed friends to support me and encourage me to get better not to keep me in an unhealthy state of mind.

As the months flew by, I gained more insight within myself that I had ever had. I realized that I had been punishing myself and my loved ones rather than those who harmed me. I realized they didn't deserve so much power over me anymore and as long as I continued to hurt myself, I was allowing them to control every aspect of my life. I lost a lot because of my self-injury. I left nursing school and I drove a wedge between my family that I never thought I could get back. I hurt my nieces and nephew each time they saw my scars. I scared my partner more times than I could count. I finally realized in order to have these things in my life; I had to choose to stop injuring. I had injured for so long that I didn't know of any other way to go on with my daily living. I was my self-injury for a very long time and my worst enemy. I got so sick of being "sick" that I didn't know how else to be. It took me moving to another county to get better.

I didn't just wake-up one morning and stop injuring. It required a lot of hard work. It meant therapy and medication. I used my impulse logs when I needed them and I took things minute by minute if I had to in order to get through the day. It wasn't easy but I wanted to be free from my self-injury and I was willing to do whatever it took to stop. I kept a journal when I had really bad days and did collages when I was really angry. Most of all I relied on myself for the strength to battle my own demons. With the help of these tools, I was able to gain a stronger hold on having an injury free life. If I had never done my impulse control logs or went to therapy, I would still be injuring. Even today I use my tools because some days are just like the very first day out of treatment. Everyone has a rotten day but you have to know how to tackle the issue in order to survive it.

The only thing I ever wanted in my life was a child of my own. However, as long as I stayed sick, I could never have a child. It wouldn't be fair or a safe environment to raise a child in. Today, I am in the process of trying to adopt a child with my partner. I don't know if it will ever happen, but I can tell you that I am a lot closer today at reaching my dream than I was 15 months ago. Dreaming of having a child of my own one day is one of the reasons I stopped injuring. I want a child more than anything, even my self-injury. It took a long time to be able to say that, but today, I say it with pride.

For the first time in my life I have stability and security. I have a partner that loves me and not my illness. She doesn't expect me to stay sick, rather encourages me to go back to school or do whatever it is my heart desires. I am finally content with my life for the most part and I look forward to each day as if it is a new beginning. Fifteen months ago I never would have seen myself living an injury free life or being alive for that matter. Today I am grateful to be here and I look at myself with pride because I know it wasn't easy to stop injuring after so many years.

Through my journey from self-injury and other unhealthy behaviors, I have come to question certain aspects of life. I was always curious why others choose to stay unhealthy rather than making a life full of love and happiness. Even though I have been through many battles I am unable to understand. For months now I have pondered why a person chooses to stay sick. Why do they act out only to get people to respond to them in some way or another? Whether it is healthy or unhealthy doesn't matter rather than the fact someone gave them the attention. What about all of the chaos? How does a person benefit from it? Why are others so quick to baby them? I have made many mistakes in my life. I have chosen to stay sick at times when others around me couldn't fathom why. I have nearly destroyed my life and until I realized I was more than the scars on my body, I could not get better. I battled bulimia to a point where I could have died. I have starved my body in punishment for things done as a child. I have injured so many times because I was the victim and I was angry. However, there comes a time when you have to take responsibility for yourself. There comes a time when you must realize being a victim runs your life rather than makes things all better.

I am not perfect by any means, but I work hard on my recovery. I always thought I could understand when a person chooses to stay sick and engage in destructive behaviors. However, that is no longer the case. I don't understand. I don't understand how someone chooses to stay stuck in a life that hurts them. Yes, I still have nightmares and I still have a hard time with my childhood, but I am in counseling working towards a healthier state of mind. I have come to realize that nothing entitles me to continue to hurt myself. The more I hurt and ruin my life, the more power I give the people who have hurt me. When I hurt myself I hurt those around me and myself. Nothing justifies that hurt. Not even the hurt inflicted upon me when I was a small child. I chose to no longer give those who have harmed me power because I know I deserve so much more than to hurt myself. Why can't other people see that? Why do others chose to stay stuck and live their life in a spiral? I thought I understood because I have been there, but now I am on the other side. I want a brighter future and I want a life that's mine and not justified by those who hurt me. I have tried to understand from where I have been and where I am today. I come back to the same place though. I find myself wanting to get better and staying better because I need it for myself. I have seen so much here and it really frustrates me. What good are people really doing for another person who is willing to stay stuck? What purpose does it serve for the person who is enabling the person who is stuck? Think about it.

Susan Sours

While there's life there's hope.
—Cicero

It was the day before Thanksgiving 1999 when I arrived at S.A.F.E. My husband and five year old daughter drove me all the way there and turned around and drove all the way home. Talk about hard! I ended up being at S.A.F.E. for my birthday and Christmas. I had a lot of guilt. I had never really thought about what my injuring might be doing to them or the rest of my family. They all tried to be as supportive as they could, but I think they were as confused as I was at times.

Even though I had come to S.A.F.E. voluntarily for help, I still couldn't believe I might be giving up self-injury. It was how I was getting by. It was getting me through the flashbacks, anger, and confusion. I had gotten so use to making people believe I was alright I started to believe it myself. Talk about confused. If I was alright, how come I was so torn up inside? I remember feeling like I was about to explode, but wanting so much to appear as if I were in complete control. How was I going to find a way to release that turmoil without self-injury? It was agony. I had so many feelings and emotions flying around inside of me I just didn't know how to express them.

The staff at S.A.F.E. was amazing. They could see right through my facade. My act didn't fool them at all and even though I was a bit ticked off by that, it was exactly what I needed. I never would have believed I would be putting so much trust in so many strangers. A lot of my walls started coming down. I could gradually see that they truly cared and I wasn't going to be left to fall through the cracks.

As caring as the staff was, they were just as tough too. Everyone was assigned their own primary staff member for going over writing assignments. These were the most important S.A.F.E. tools for me. I really had to take a good hard look inside myself. Who was I? Where did I come from? And what had I been through? For the first time I was putting honest feelings down on paper and I was going to share them with another person—a person I barely knew. It wasn't long before I was opening up. These assignments were some of the hardest yet rewarding work I've ever done. I still use writing today to help me get things out, things I can't express verbally. It made it possible for me to develop a personal relationship and see that it can be safe.

Being with my peer group almost twenty-four hours a day proved to be a learning experience in itself. All of us had been through so much of the same stuff that it made it easier to trust each other. I was slowly learning that it was "ok" to share emotions and even express them. I didn't have to hold everything in. It wasn't always comfortable to feel, but it was actually a relief to get it all out. That was probably the second most important thing I learned at S.A.F.E.. Just knowing I wasn't the only one doing this, I wasn't crazy or bazaar. After shutting so many people out of my life and keeping so many secrets, it was unbelievable to know that just talking could lift such a burden from my shoulders. I developed a close bond with them. It was incredibly hard to say goodbye.

I took a lot of risk while I was at S.A.F.E.. I opened myself up to criticisms in order to grow. I knew I wasn't perfect when I went there, but I sure was in denial about being in control. They made me realize I was hurting my family with self-injury. I never thought I was actually hurting them. I guess I never really thought about what it was doing to them at all. I just wanted them to except it. I didn't see how selfish I was being at the time. I was pushing my family away because I couldn't self-injure and care about them at the same time.

After five weeks my husband and daughter came to take me home. I felt like a different person and I knew right away when I saw them things were changing. Leaving everyone behind was very hard, but I was looking forward to getting home. It was scary and some of the staff thought I would go home and injure again, but I proved them wrong—at least for a little while. I did really well for the first couple of months. I stayed in touch with one of my peers quite often. It's been almost five years and we're still e-mailing and staying in touch. She's been a big source of strength for me. We seem to know when the other might need some support. The first year was really rough, but I survived. My other source of support was a wonderful therapist and an incredibly caring doctor who unfortunately past away this year. I learned alot from him and I'm trying to carry that over into my relationship with my new doctor.

My daughter's getting ready to turn ten. I can't believe how fast she's grown. My husband and I try to be as honest with her as possible. I want her to know she can come to us with anything and not be afraid. I haven't quite figured out how to discuss self-injury with her though. I just want her to have the self-confidence I didn't when I was her age.

I still have my ups and downs, but I've been injury free for four years now. S.A.F.E. wasn't magic; it took a lot of hard work on my part. I would recommend it to anyone struggling with self-injury. The work never ends, but you wouldn't believe how good it feels to have a choice now.

I'm extremely thankful to all the staff at S.A.F.E. for their guidance.

Shelley Frank

It is easy to live for others: everybody does. I call on you to live for yourselves.
—Ralph Waldo Emerson

When I walked into the hospital that first day, I silently told myself that this was my last chance. If I blow it here, there is no hope for me. I would love to encouragingly say that the second I started treatment all my fears dissipated, but that would be a lie. As a matter of fact, my fears greatly increased before I got to the point of acceptance. I had been to many doctors and treatment programs before. The main motto I heard was "Stop it", "You're only hurting yourself", or the ever popular "Just try harder". These things were not only unhelpful, but also counteractive. I came out of all of these feeling more like a freak and a failure than before. In S.A.F.E. I learned that self-injury is not the only problem I had. It was a side effect of the unresolved issues and emotions I was faced with.

One of my worst fears upon entering the program was that I would become just another statistic. It wasn't so much that I wanted to be singled out or different. I just know that I am my own individual person. I was afraid that I would be lumped into the category of a self-injurer and my treatment would be based solely on that. I was shocked to find that self-injury was not the main focus of the program, but instead what the causes behind the action are. While it was a group-based program, I got the individual attention and treatment I needed to succeed. I look back on my time at S.A.F.E. with a sort of weary pride. It was hard work, very hard work. The talking about things I didn't want to talk about, spilling all my secrets, and logging was all hard, but all of it helped me different times in the future.

I went into S.A.F.E. a scared, self-loathing injurer, whose main goal in life was to make it through the next day. I now lead a normal life. I go to school, am involved in many different programs, am comfortable with myself, and most importantly, I haven't self-injured since I started the program. I still break out the logs when I'm having a rough day, but the coping skills and reasoning I learned at S.A.F.E. has kept me going through some of the hardest issues in my life. I would recommend to anyone dealing with this issue to look into S.A.F.E.. It truly changed my life and I am forever grateful. The thing is you must be ready to get better. You can't be making up your mind while you're there. If you give it all you've got, it will be one of the most rewarding experiences of your life.

Amanda Rogers.

The fearful unbelief is unbelief in yourself.
—Thomas Carlyle

It's called: "Hoy se Camina Seguro" (which means in Spanish: Today We Walk Safely)

Today we walk safely through the furrows of history,
Measuring time with the steps
of one who has just learned to stand.
We create the momentum of lifetimes through grated faith

Soon we will look to gods that have reappeared, the story
of these few years they have slept
will be lost, as one grain of sand
is lost, dropped along the lengths of Varadero; Grain fades

Into grain, recalls the beach made new in restless shiftings
and somehow, before we've drowned
in mortal apathy, we'll have
Forgotten. This is our prayer. This is the evidence

Of our hundred hopes. The seconds paint the way towards citrine
Colored houses, and the ground
our fathers cultivated—salve
made thick to soothe the wreck of where we've been; A land condensed

To these meager things: the silent throngs of allegory,
Gods unshackled from their rest,
The faith we'll choose, as men, to hand
to our future, and the furrows in which to plant a new day

Take care,
Juliette

People must help one another; it is nature's law
—Jean De La Fontaine

S.A.F.E.

Once caged by pain
I have found a choice
Once muted by fear
I have found a voice

Choices are not answers
And a voice is not a song
But there is melody in choosing
Having been silent so long

Pain is not abolished
Nor even held at bay
I have not conquered fear
Nor turned the night to day

But I have learned to feel
And in feeling still survive
Embracing pain and letting go
Is the dance of being alive

CB

From small beginnings comes great things.
—Proverb

To Choose Happiness

My life is so very different now. I haven't injured in over ten years. I actually had to sit down and figure that out. In the beginning I could have told you to the day how long it had been since I injured. Now it is such a distant part of my life that I couldn't remember how long it had been. In fact, that was my only reluctance in writing this. I no longer identify myself as a self-injurer or even as an ex-self-injurer. It just isn't a relevant part of my life. But if telling my story can help someone else find the hope and courage to choose happiness, it is worth revisiting the ghosts of the past.

I began injuring as a young teenager. At least, that is the first time I recall deliberately causing myself harm. Looking further back, I probably engaged in behaviors that could be considered self-injurious from a much younger age. I had no clear idea of why I engaged in this behavior, but I had a sense that my feelings were "too big" to be contained. Injuring was somehow a way of releasing those feelings that I was unable to express any other way. Because of the abusive and incestuous environment in which I grew up, it was unsafe to express feelings in a more conventional manner.

At first self injury was a cry for the chaos in my life to be discovered. It was a cry that went unnoticed. I became secretive about my behavior. It wasn't until my early 30's that the behavior became so out of control that it was no longer possible to keep it hidden. In 1987, I was hospitalized for depression. That hospitalization began a spiral of injury, depression, suicidal ideation, and eating disorders that was to continue for a number of years. No one seemed to know how to help, and I certainly had no idea how to help myself. I was told that I was chronically mentally ill and could look forward to a life of institutionalization.

In the spring of 1992, I read the book *Secret Survivors* by E. Sue Blume. The chapter on self-injury made more sense to me than anything my current care providers had ever said. In the back of the book was a phone number that would eventually change my life. From the patient phone of a mental hospital I called 1-800-DONTCUT and requested information about the S.A.F.E. program. When the information came, I tossed it on my psychiatrist's desk and said "Get me into this program." To his credit he made the call and started the ball rolling.

By May of 1992, I was an inpatient in the S.A.F.E. program. I spent 30 days learning the tools, attending groups, doing writing assignments and being the "good" patient. It was only in the last week of the program, that I began to let down some of my defenses to take a look at how I continued to live my life. I was unable to clearly face the abusiveness of my marriage and how unhealthy that relationship was. I returned home, knowing the tools, but not yet committed to making them work for me. I returned to teaching in the fall, still injury-free, but still desperately unhappy. By October, I was injuring again. I returned to Chicago and the hospital.

This time I had to look squarely at my life and make some changes. It was the beginning of a long road to recovery. I left my abusive marriage. I admitted my sexual orientation to myself for the first time and I decided to move to Chicago permanently and found an apartment. My ex-husband retained custody of my children. Surely that was enough life change for anyone. Now that I had made all of these changes, everything was supposed to magically get all better, right? Wrong!

I continued in therapy in Chicago. I participated in outpatient S.A.F.E. groups. I knew all of the right words. I had wonderful insight and could easily see what everyone else needed to do to get well but I continued injuring. Some part of this program just wasn't sinking in for me and I couldn't understand it. After all I was smart, I wrote beautiful, touching answers to all of the writing assignments and I knew this program by heart. So what was the problem?

Much later I would look back and make this analogy: My car keeps breaking down. I find a wonderful class in simple car mechanics and repair. I go to class faithfully and learn everything they have to teach me. I buy all of the best tools. I lock my toolbox carefully in the trunk of my car. I never take out the tools to perform the basic maintenance on my car. Low and behold, it breaks down again. Stupid class! Lousy tools! It never occurred to me that I would actually have to pick them up and use them.

There finally came a point in my life where my behavior began costing me more than I cared to pay. After nine months of not injuring, living in a beautiful apartment with a roommate to help with the expenses, I injured for the last time. Because of my behavior, I lost my roommate, lost my apartment and nearly lost all of the few friendships I had managed to establish since moving to Chicago. I was hospitalized again. During that time, Karen Contario spoke with me. She said that perhaps she had been wrong about me. Perhaps this was the best I could do. Suddenly I was angry. How dare she say such a thing to me I'd show her. I could choose to not injure, just watch me.

It's been more than ten years since that conversation. In the beginning, I chose not to injure because I didn't want her words to be true. As time went by, I chose not to injure because I saw that it really was a choice. It was this simple and most powerful tool that I had failed to understand. I could make the choice not to injure. I had thought, in some skewed way, that injuring gave me control. It didn't. It sent my life spinning out of control. Choices are what give us control and I had the choice not to injure.

Once I stopped injuring, the rest of my recovery could begin. Therapy became much more effective as I was no longer covering my feelings with my injurious behavior. If I could choose not to injure, I could also choose to get well in other ways. It wasn't easy. It wasn't quick. But it has been worth it. After two years of intensive therapy in a partial hospitalization program, I returned to work for the first time in years. I started slow, in a job that helped me to feel good about myself, but didn't pay terribly well. When I decided that I was worth more than I was being paid, I moved on.

In the beginning, I had to make the choice not to injure over and over again. Sometimes I had to make it many times in a single day. As my time and recovery went on, I was faced with a direct choice less and less often. I began to make other positive choices. I chose to be a functioning adult. I chose to open myself to the possibility of relationships. I chose happiness and found that I no longer had to choose not to injure—it was simply not an option. When the occasional thought crossed my mind, during times of stress, I chose not to entertain the thought. Dwelling on those thoughts would be to invite the possibility of injuring back into my life. Now I find that even in times of stress, the option rarely occurs to me. On those very rare occasions, the thought is more along the line of, "At one time I might have injured over this, but I can't imagine doing that now."

As I said at the outset, my life is so very different now. I met a wonderful woman about six years ago and fell in love. We will celebrate our fifth anniversary later this month. We bought a house together a year and half ago and are living a quiet life in the suburbs of Chicago. I am a tenured teacher at an elementary school. I love my job and am respected by the people with whom I work. I have a great relationship with both of my children despite the turmoil caused by my injuring and illness during their childhood. I no longer have symptoms of severe depression or eating disorders. I continue to see my therapist twice a month for "maintenance." Life still has its ups and downs, of course. But now, most days, I choose happiness.

CB

Health is not a condition of matter, but of mind.
—Mary Baker Eddy

My story of recovery comes from an interesting perspective. I survived three years nearly injury free until a few months ago. At that point, I suffered a major relapse and returned to S.A.F.E.. I came home about six weeks ago and feel, once again, like a newborn in recovery. Many of the problems I face are the same but some are new. This time around I am living in a new city with my husband, not my parents. My therapist and psychiatrist are the same. I will base my story on my three previous years of recovery. Those years were mostly healthy as a specific incident triggered my relapse, not a culmination of events over those three years. I imagine much of what helped me then is what is going to help me now, and hopefully can help others.

I entered S.A.F.E. the first time extremely reluctant and hospitalized for self-injury and a major suicide attempt. My parents were not going to let me come home and the hospital was not going to release me to them anyway. I saw S.A.F.E. as the only place I could go.

Despite myself, I worked very hard and made huge changes. I remember struggling with relationships with the other girls on the unit. I struggled with taking responsibility for myself and for letting others take responsibility for themselves. Of course I was just playing out my relationships with my family members. With the help of staff and some very understanding friends on the unit, I worked out these conflicts and was ready to apply what I learned to my life at home. Reading what the staff and fellow patients wrote in my *Bodily Harm* book, I entered S.A.F.E. a rough, unpredictable young woman with drastic mood swings. To them, I left a stronger woman who took an honest look at herself and was able to stand up for herself and leave martyrdom behind.

I left S.A.F.E. as a 24-year-old professional woman to live at home with my parents. My first and foremost priority was to repair this relationship and to stand up for myself. I play the caretaker role in the family. Most of the time, I am burdened with the feelings of my alcoholic father or martyr mother. Most of the time my needs came last, I had to learn to put my needs first. Often times, this felt like it was the wrong thing to do. I felt as if telling my dad he was making me feel guilty or that I did not want to watch a movie with him was betraying him, or that he would hate me or abandon me. Still, I could not let him walk all over me. Sometimes he listened to me and sometimes he didn't. The hard part was to realize the value in asking for what I needed and not hurting myself whether I got it or not. Talking to my mom was easier. She eventually grew more sensitive to my needs and to this day, asks me for less. My dad will probably never "get it." I will probably always feel invisible when I am around him, a huge trigger for me to hurt myself. I learned that giving myself a voice keeps me from being invisible, whether he acknowledges me or not.

One of the most important things to me when I left S.A.F.E. was a S.A.F.E. Aftercare group I participated in. I understand that this was a rare opportunity and no longer exists. My point is that, early in recovery, when I wasn't necessarily motivated solely for myself, I felt responsible to stay safe, honest and present for the group. I made connections with each and every member of the group. I felt connected to other people unlike the connections I had with my coworkers. The group was a forum to share feelings, struggles, and relationships. I participated in this weekly group for a year and a half. While this group may not be available, I encourage anyone to find a group—AA, NA, OA, AL-ANON, AL-ATEEN, ANAD that applies to them and make a commitment to go. In addition to the support of a group, I had the support of the same therapist I've had for six years. I never stopped going to therapy. I also saw the same psychiatrist and had the support of medication.

S.A.F.E. taught me to take responsibility for my actions. It may sound ridiculous, but I had no idea that by hurting myself, I was hurting the people who loved me too. For months, I used Impulse Control Logs. I found the column on consequences particularly helpful. I realize now that my behaviors have consequences. My behaviors affected myself as well as others. My eating disorder and self-injury have prevented me from performing my best at jobs, from sustaining lasting relationships, and from building trust with others. Before I was in S.A.F.E., I was hospitalized twice for an eating disorder. Until then, I had not considered food restriction or purging self-injury. I used my logs for eating disorder impulses. To this day, I am free of my eating disorder.

Another thing that changed my life that might not be available to everyone was my dog, Benny. My family had been living without a pet for several months. In the months after S.A.F.E., I researched different breeds of dogs. Finally, I found Benny, an English springer spaniel puppy. Benny changed my life. This little creature's life was my responsibility. He relied on me for food, water, walks, play, naps, treats, toys, training, and going outside. I had to take responsibility for myself in order to take responsibility for him. I couldn't sleep away the day when Benny needed to be walked, fed, trained and played with. To this day, Benny is one of the sweetest dogs you'll ever meet. I take responsibility for that.

Even when I feel low, I feel good knowing that I raised a great dog. I could go on and on about the value of having a pet. I am a dog groomer and work for a nationwide chain of pet stores. If you can get a pet, I think it's one of the best things you can do.

I can't possibly write all that helped me in my recovery. For me, a good support system was crucial. I found that through my therapist, psychiatrist and S.A.F.E. Aftercare Group. I was also fortunate enough to find the man I was to marry. Another important thing is to use words instead of actions. I had to learn to speak up to my parents. I am still working on that one and have to learn to speak up to my husband. The key is taking responsibility. I thought my injuries had no consequences. I thought wrong. Of course, healthy distractions, like a pet, can be helpful too. I wish everyone well on his or her road to recovery. It has its ups and downs, as I am living proof of, but there is always hope.

Janelle Warnick

The heart has its reason, which reason does not know.
—Blaise Pascal

I am a recovered self-injurer. After all that I've dealt with over the past few years, I can't believe that I'm even saying that. Beating self-injury was one of the hardest things I've ever done. For close to ten years I used self-harm to cope with my intense emotional pain. I won't lie and say that I regret putting myself through that torment. I've learned a lot from what I've been through. I think that suffering makes a person stronger. Though I'm certainly not recommending it, self-injury might have been the only thing that kept me alive. I'll never know, but I am, for a certainty, a better person for it.

I've always felt guilty for "having problems." By all outward appearances, I've had a wonderful life. I have two parents who live together and love each other. I have two younger sisters who have always been my friends. I grew up in an Elysian middle-class suburb. I was the brightest kid in class. I had friends, pets, and a social life. To this day I have a hard time putting my finger on what went wrong. So instead of focusing on the reasons behind my self injury, I try to maintain a clear view of my positive future—a future without self-harm.

I had been injuring for about three years before anyone ever realized something was wrong. I wore long sleeves and pants in the middle of the summer. I kept my life to myself, was highly self-controlled and enormously secretive. No one knew my pain. I did, however, keep extensive journals from the age of 12, when my problems first started, until the age of 16. It was the discovery of these journals that finally brought my problems to light. My parents, who discovered my writings and therefore my injury, were horrified at what had become of me in my teenage years. They couldn't explain it, couldn't control it, and couldn't understand it. So they drove me right over to the emergency room, where I was deemed crazy and shipped over to the university mental hospital.

In the psychiatric ward, my problem got worse instead of better. The supervision was poor, the help was sparse, and I was hell-bent on self-destruction. I was prematurely released from the hospital two weeks later with a diagnosis of major depression and a handful of psychotropic drug prescriptions. The drugs did nothing for me. I was severely depressed and now increasingly suicidal. My life was going downhill very fast and no one was there to stop me. I felt alone, despondent, and bitter.

After another unsuccessful two-week psychiatric hospital visit at 19 years old, I decided it was time to take my care into my own hands. Hospitals, therapists, and psychiatrists, especially those unknowledgeable about self-injury, just weren't helping and were even making things worse. I think I innately wanted to live. Not just to live, but to thrive and be happy. So I took action.

An avid reader, I bought every book on self-injury I could find. There weren't many out there, but one I did find struck a chord—*Bodily Harm*. It seemed sincere and accurate. I had never read anything that described my feelings so much. Most importantly, I learned that I wasn't alone. All this time I thought that I was the only one in the world who hurt herself to feel better. But now I knew that not only was there other people out there like me, there were people who understood people like me. I was so relieved I wept.

I worked up the courage to show the book to my parents, and I told them that I wanted to be a part of the S.A.F.E. Alternatives program. They were supportive and I think they were as desperate as I was. This seemed like the answer. They didn't put up a fight about the cost of the program, but I had to give up a lot to attend. My entire family was planning a trip to Italy right around the time I had hoped to go to S.A.F.E., but I knew I would not have enjoyed a vacation. I wouldn't have enjoyed anything until I got help. So while they packed their bags for a glorious three-week *vacanza Italiano*, I packed my little suitcase for yet another hospital stay, only this time and for the first time it my life, it was voluntary. One less stamp in my passport, but I hoped it would lead to a lifetime free of more scars.

I arrived at the hospital in Chicago wearing long sleeves and long pants, covered from head to toe; unsure of what I would find when I got there. I was dumbfounded to encounter a half-dozen other girls with scars like mine. The camaraderie alone put me immediately at ease. I could relax and I did. For the rest of my time there, I wore short sleeves. I hadn't been able to do that in many years. For the first time in my life, I was able to trust my peers, and the people who were trying to help me. It truly was safe in every sense of the word.

Although I don't feel that I ever came to an accurate conclusion as to the root of my problem, I was able to identify the feelings that led up to my self-injury. I was able to learn new ways of dealing with negative emotions. For the first time in as long as I could remember, I was able to talk through my feelings instead of bottling them up, only to be released in an explosive, violent manner later. I benefited from the structure of the program. I benefited from the friendships I established and from the lines of communication that were opened. The S.A.F.E. Alternatives program literally saved my life.

Admittedly, I had a pendulum-style relapse after I left S.A.F.E.. Being at home again was so different than being in an emotionally safe environment. I fell back into my old patterns of not talking and injuring to cope with my feelings, but eventually I came back around. I remembered and applied all that I had learned—mainly, how to use words instead of self-harm—and I made a complete recovery.

My life now is right where I've always wanted it to be. I finally am able to hold down a steady job that I love. I started college this year, a little late, but better now than never. I've rebuilt a trusting relationship with my parents and most of all, I've gained strength and self respect. I still am constantly reminded of my past, but I can finally hold my head high and say with confidence, "I am a recovered self-injurer." and darn proud of it, too.

Juliette

Many hands make light work.
—Proverb

Open Book by Dana D. Read

If I close my eyes and remember the first few minutes I was at S.A.F.E. I can still remember the feelings that dropped from my head right to the bottom of my stomach with a big thud. I looked over my shoulder to say goodbye to the friend who had brought me and I knew that she had felt the thud with me. I imagine I would have cried if I had it left in me by then. The doors locked behind her and I had a sudden lack of breath as I sat down with the others who were doing art therapy and slowly brought my eyes over to the group around me.

Going to S.A.F.E. was like opening a book that I had only heard about in bits and pieces—a very long book, which I am still trying to read. I went with the vaguest idea of who I was and what I needed. I've spent a large part of my life wishing I could melt into the walls around me. Not getting in anyone's way so that I could just live my life without having to explain. I grew up in a family of five starting out in the Southwest United States and through several moves spent the largest part of my childhood in Ohio. In a family of left brained thinkers, I was the only right brain thinker "Dana-logic" my sister calls it. While this could have been viewed as a great gift, being different often caused me great consternation and loneliness trying to explain my opinions and decisions. Also, being an introvert, I did not find it easy to make friends, but I usually had one or two good friends around. I enjoyed activities with the church youth group called the "Pink Pig". I clung to the knowledge that God was with me even when no one else could be or would be. I was not a good student and I was an exceptionally average athlete in a family of tennis, hockey, soccer, and golf players. It was in my art classes that I felt at home and able to communicate. Fortunately, I was able to take art classes all the way through school and finally went to do my undergraduate degree in fine arts.

After a very traumatic event in my third grade year, my struggle with self-injury began. By the time I went to Girl Scout camp in sixth grade I had the nickname "Dana-don't-bruise-your-body-Read". At this time, I began my struggle with an eating disorder.

While I was in college, I had a good friend try and get me to see a counselor about my eating disorder. Unhappy and angry with my friend, I finally agreed to go at least once. I may have gone one or two times more than that, but I don't think I went much longer. I didn't want to change. I didn't think I was hurting anyone. And it helped me, so I thought, face my life every day. I didn't think anyone would ever understand how much I needed my eating disorder. Having an eating disorder was bad enough, but if someone found out about the injuring I was sure they would think I was crazy. I had never heard of anyone else doing these things I was doing. In my own head I thought I was crazy. I just didn't want others to confirm that for me.

I was in a place of desperation by the time I called S.A.F.E.. I entered the program on May 1st and had been seeing a therapist for a little over a year until earlier that March when she had told me that she couldn't see me any more. My life was so unmanageable and that was spilling over into every area and relationship in my life. I needed someone who I could call in an emergency, rarely, even in the middle of the night, and that was not her. She was not prepared to be that available.

My disappointment with this situation was palpable. I felt it hang in the air around me as a cloud of rejection. Every reason others had ever left or ended relationships with me came back to haunt me. I often suffered from nightmares which only intensified the situation. I tried to see it in terms of her healthiness and being able to set boundaries. I even thanked her for telling me instead of letting it go on and building resentments. I told her I was glad she knew her limits of what she thought she could handle and went to see the new therapist she recommended. Even though this proved to be a very growing relationship for me, I had a constant fear of being told that I was also too much for her to handle and so kept certain parts of myself well hidden.

I had begun to deal with aspects of sexual abuse and other childhood hurts before I entered S.A.F.E.. Some of those closest around me knew of my self-destructive coping methods. I wanted to stop and knew I needed to in order for my life to change from this unmanageable mess, a big knot of yarn where the beginning and end are hard to pull out. I needed a beginning and wanted an end. Unfortunately, I had no idea how to find either.

Again I made another error in judgment and after getting rid of all my self-injury tools went upstairs and used something from the Pastor's kitchen in the house where I lived. I had no right to use anything of theirs, giving them a feeling of unsafety in their own home where they were raising five kids. I was taken to the emergency room that night by the other girl renting a room downstairs and treated like a deadly criminal in the emergency room, with a police guard, drug tests, endless psych evaluations, and no help in the end except a reminder to go see my therapist the next day when they eventually released me at 3 a.m. I believe this was actually the event that precipitated the change in therapists. The first therapist having not liked being awakened so many times during the night, I can't blame her, but I did need her help.

That week after a friend had been telling me about S.A.F.E. for a few weeks, I finally called and found out the name of their book, *Bodily Harm* by Karen Contario and Wendy Lader, Ph.D. Karen suggested I read the *Tool Box* section. I felt as if someone just handed me answers to questions I'd had for years. A real tool box. It was with somewhat of a reckless abandon that I began those essays and used the logs. I found myself unable to process them once a week with my therapist with everything else going on though. We were still doing quite a bit of crisis management and we never really got to looking at what I had written.

Over about two weeks I knew that I had to go to S.A.F.E. and get whatever I could from the program. I called S.A.F.E. and spoke to someone named Carrie that day and asked about an outpatient program. Unfortunately, the outpatient program consisted of a once a week therapy group and I didn't think that would be enough for me. In a week I called her back and asked about inpatient. She said I was only the third person to call about outpatient and then decide to go inpatient.

It was one of the best decisions of my life, but scary as hell. During my time there, it was, as I said, as if I opened a book for the first time, the book of my life. I started to put things together and look at the big picture of where I had been and note what it was that I wanted in the future, even if for then I was too scared to try and get much out of it. At least my hope started returning.

Living behind locked doors for two weeks had me in a panic at times. At other times I felt a sense of security I had lacked for many years. What was the most valuable thing I took from my time at S.A.F.E.? I am surprised to learn, looking back now, just what that was. I reread my journal and looked at all my drawings. The central theme I found was my desire to be real, authentic, to put away images and masks, and just "be". I wanted to find my voice and know who the real Dana was.

I expected to look back and see how hard I worked to stop injuring, to stop hating myself, and to stop finding everything wrong with me. But I read the story of the *Velveteen Rabbit,* early in my stay at S.A.F.E.. I see in my notes and journal entries a desire to be genuine. Where I hated my body, where I hated who I was, where I was angry or tired or sad, and where I was content or playful, I wanted to be fully in that moment. I wanted to give myself permission to feel those things and acknowledge them. Unfortunately, in those days, I still had this idea that if I acknowledged something to be true, I thought that I had fully dealt with it and had a tendency to shelve it, therefore not really getting to the core issues. But as I said, this was only the start of the book—a very long book I am still reading.

I wish that I had spoken to some people who had gone to S.A.F.E. a couple of years before I did, before I left the hospital. I wish I had realized that life was not going to be all "fixed" once I left S.A.F.E.. I'm not sure what I expected. But what I got, I was not expecting.

I left S.A.F.E. with a whole bunch of new issues all opened up. For one of the first times I had acknowledged how deeply I struggled with anorexia. I had told the whole group that I had been sexually assaulted as a child. I talked about the communication dysfunction of my family of origin and my longing to feel like I belonged somewhere just as I am. I spoke of my relationship with an orphan in India that taught me to love profoundly and the grief I faced in leaving that nation after seven years for a fiancé in the United States who did not love me. I spoke about how he not only did not love me, but was spiritually and emotionally abusive and how that affected my relationship with my God. I faced rejection again when I returned home to the Pastor's family I lived with in their basement and was asked to look for another place to live. They were not sure how to trust me and I was home frequently so that must have been uncomfortable for them plus I no longer had a job. Since I was not injuring, my eating disorder was out of control and I was not altogether sure there was anything I could do about it. To top it all off, my family whom I was not in close communication with at that time was frequently in town preparing for my brothers upcoming wedding in October of 2o01. Boy did I feel overwhelmed.

I was fortunate to be able to attend the S.A.F.E. Aftercare group in Chicago. The leader of this group continues to be one of the most influential people in my life. Her compassion and understanding for those of us in that group helped me find a place where I mattered and could continue that "velveteen rabbit" process of becoming more real. I found this a challenging group and a place of accountability. While I rarely if ever spoke of my eating disorder, I did find accountability for continuing in recovery from self-injury for two entire years. After years and years of one self destructive act after another, I celebrated this victory often—every month in fact. At my one-year anniversary, several very good friends and I went to dinner at the Russian Tea Room downtown for a fancy dinner and a walk around downtown. I still wear the necklace they gave me as a reminder of their love and support and that victory is possible.

Going to S.A.F.E. was just the beginning. I never imagined that I'd ever have to seek inpatient treatment again. I thought I was done with that forever. Certainly, financially I was done with that forever. Medical parody is such a necessity for mental health issues in our nation.

Facing me has meant going deeper and looking for that place where I can be vulnerable and authentic, genuine and real. That's the place of home for me, the place where understanding and wisdom lay. It's where I will find freedom. Along my journey, I have been fortunate to know that I have a God who walks with me every step of the way. I don't know how I would have made it this far without Him. I have found that He made me to be who I am and while it was not His plan for me to be hurt and misused or misunderstood as a child, He does promise good for those who love Him and I believe I am beginning to see that goodness.

Despite having seen the goodness of God in so many ways, I was not able to leave my eating disorder behind. Many people with good intention or the "law" of God in their hearts reminded me that I was supposed to take care of the temple of the Holy Spirit that I had been given—my body. Others prayed that I would be able to leave my "sin" behind and stop having an eating disorder. Even others accused me of choosing to live in sin by having an eating disorder. These words of condemnation wound themselves around my mind and heart over and over. I feared I would never be completely acceptable to God no matter what. This was a heavy load to carry.

I was in treatment for anorexia twice this last year. The first time I went I was so grateful to leave with my life, knowing that had I gone on as I was before treatment; I would have gravely endangered my life. Somewhere in the beginning of treatment, I began injuring again. I hated myself, I hated my body, and I wanted to destroy it. When I finally managed to allow myself to receive help and to reach out to the God I knew was always there, I found myself able to start on the road towards recovery though I still wondered why He would help someone like me who was "living in sin" with my eating disorder.

I made a lot of huge changes in my life after that, making a move to a new state, settling closer to my family after a week of family therapy to find more reconciliation and solidity to our relationships. I started school and a new job. I began looking for a new church, and tried to get to know new people. All of this while trying to stay in recovery. Perhaps it is needless to say, but I lost hold of my recovery while putting so much effort into everything else. Just to keep life going, I felt I had to put all my energy out there and I kept injuring and restricting my food to find some sense of control and organization, I suppose. Well, I know it was for a whole lot of other reasons too. These bad decisions brought me to a very sick place again.

I thought I was done with it all, no more dealing with old stuff, that I was raped when I was nine years old, that I had seen disturbing poverty and destitution in South Asia, and that I had faced spiritual and emotional abuse, that I had dealt with it. I should be able to put the rest of it in a folder and shelve it. I couldn't understand why it kept jumping up in my dreams and flashing back at me during the day. I couldn't understand my intense fears and sense of loss of control. It had felt this way before but I had already talked about it at S.A.F.E. and in therapy, in groups so someone else knew with me now, I wasn't alone, so it "shouldn't" bother me anymore. I would have willed it to be done if that were possible. But of course, it hasn't been and I am still learning to deal with it all on some levels.

It crept up on me this summer until I was living in my eating disorder and injuring regularly. I worried that God was unable to look at me or to forgive me. I tried and tried to get myself out of this downward spiral. When I realized I could not do it alone in outpatient, I checked myself into Rosewood Ranch in Wickenburg, AZ. I think I was ready this time, ready to listen, absorb, question, talk, cry, and draw it all out. I was ready to pray and wait for God to show Himself for the truth of who He is. I was ready to feel. The first time I met with the psychiatrist I told him I knew that I needed to work on my trauma issues. I knew that anyway I could, I needed to feel something about what had happened to me as a little girl, not act on it. Just feel it and see what happened. I realized later, though I've been told ever since S.A.F.E., I had never really felt the anger or the sadness I thought was supposed to be there. Not as much as I had stored up inside.

My weeks at Rosewood taught me some valuable lessons. My book was still open and it seemed like a chapter or two was going to be finished. I learned that dealing with things in my life didn't just mean acknowledging them or saying them out loud. It meant saying them, talking about them again and again, writing about them, drawing about them, crying about them, grieving them, and going outside and throwing rocks into the river bed again and again. It meant acknowledging them, accepting them, allowing them to be part of my past, and embracing them as part of what made me who I am today. It means using them and allowing them to teach me and others who are part of my life now. Not that I have to tell everyone what happened, but if I can live with a little less judgment and a little more compassion because of what I have experienced, then I have used my past for something good.

I have learned to look at my self-injury and eating disorder coping strategies as gifts for the time that they were needed. We use this stuff because it works, let's face it. For me, it helped me survive things I might not have if I didn't have them, but I don't need them anymore. I want to share with you a letter I wrote to say goodbye to my eating disorder. I wrote in it my goodbye to self-injury again too. For me they really go together. When I wasn't using one I used the other. Right now I am in recovery from both for the first time. I'll leave you with this letter:

Dear ED,

I have been so deceived by you. I have listened to your voice and trusted you. I sought you out and looked for ways to be a better follower of your ways. I was good at it, but it was never enough to take away the shame or guilt or anger. I thought I just had to try harder, lose more weight, eat less, walk more miles, block out feelings, cut, and hit to make my inadequacies and insecurities go away. You promised I'd like my body or at least tolerate it. But my insecurities only grew and my dislike, even hatred, for the body I live in only raged on.

Where was the comfort you promised when my loneliness became like a disease and followed me through the nights and days? Where was the hope of things to change each time I lost a little more or deprived myself of one more friendship? Where was the strength I was supposed to feel when my body and mind got weaker while I followed all your rules? Where was that strength when I could hardly lift my patients or make their beds or remember their requests? Where were you when I could hardly remember who I was? You were there all the time. But under that little whisper is a monster I've let run my life for way to long. You know me so well, almost better than I do, or at least you know how to push every trigger button as hard as you can. I don't expect you to stop right now, tomorrow, next week, or next month or maybe even next year. But yours is no longer the only voice to choose from. I used to feel powerful when I could deny myself things that other people needed, especially when I could take something that was mine, convince myself I did not need it, and give it to someone else, like as giving my food or clothes to beggars in India. But now, giving you up, I no longer feel powerful. I feel powerless at times. I never feel comfortably empty, I feel uncomfortably full. I am scared of your little whispers and critical, judgmental comments. I've been pulled back by you so many times. There are times I fear finding you waiting for me on my plate or sitting next to me at a meal. But, again, yours is not the only voice. I want a real life in recovery more than anything else.

I want open, honest, vulnerable relationships. I want to recognize your voice and use mine back. There are so many places to see and interesting things to do, I don't want to be held back by fear or because to go would mean eating out with a friend or someone seeing my scars. I want to embrace each day and live in abundance in the present—enjoying a swing, a sunset, a walk, cool weather, the promises of rainbows, and all kinds of things. I have let those things slip by while concentrating on you and avoiding feeling anything. I want to embrace my humanity, my imperfections, my feelings, thoughts, remembrances, and the world around me, friendships, and so much more. You stand in my way.

I commit myself to fighting against you as hard as I can as long as necessary while I live my life. I got some things from you for a while, things that made my survival possible, but it doesn't work anymore. I know sometimes the tightness of my clothing or the shape of my body will tempt me back into your ways. Feelings and circumstances may give me an overwhelming amount of emotion which may also try to win me back over to you. But I am going to fight you. I don't need you anymore—you are hurting me. LET GO!! Goodbye, ED and SI. Never come back.

Written with love for myself,

Dana

Hope is a waking dream.
—Aristotle

I am a living miracle. I should not have survived my past, but I have. If I can live, survive, and thrive so can you. It is possible. There *is* life after self-injury. Everybody wrote me off as a lost cause, a hopeless case. I am not sure where I should begin my story, but I know for certain that it has no end. My history was similar to most of the others who were in the program with me in 2000: years of suppressed pain, memories, and anger that I thought could never be expressed, let alone looked at.

I truly do no know how it began. Self-injury had played a role in my life until five years ago. My life was a mess. My eldest sister scared me with her screaming and yelling. I was just a little kid and did not understand all the conflict between her and my parents. She did not treat me or my siblings well either. My childhood was very confusing and conflicting. I felt so alone, worthless, and most of all unlovable. I learned early how to get the love I craved within the walls of psychiatric units, where I resided for months at a time. For 15 years, I was in and out of psychiatric hospitalization until I found the S.A.F.E. Alternatives Program in 2000.

While I didn't know what was to hit me that cold January, I entered the program with my walls firm around me; walls I didn't even know could be knocked down. My facades were many, and my denial in place, but they all saw through my many facades and the walls to my pain were broken down to my very soul. It was only after a week in the program that I sobbed. I remember sitting on the floor by the telephone, weeping, at the realization of how out of control the life I led was. The work in this program was constant and rigorous, yet it was the first time in my life that I truly felt that I got any help. After 15 years in and out of psychiatric hospitals, I was ready to change. I worked hard in the program and faced my inner most conflicts and the tears came. So many feelings were aroused; feelings I had suppressed for so long and now the real challenge began—learning how to sit with my feelings no matter how difficult. The S.A.F.E. program in combination with my willingness and determination led me into combat against self-injury itself. Part of the determination was not to let the ones who hurt me have victories over me anymore. The willingness came from the exhaustion of a life filled with crisis management. It was time I got peace. Not only from my past, but also from the life I led. I was determined that after 15 years this would be my last psychiatric hospitalization and it has been.

It wasn't easy leaving the program. At times I had to study my *Injury Alternatives* and just do them to remain safe. The work really began upon leaving. Learning to cope in the real world was quite a challenge. Creating a new identity than the "identified patient" has been a hard, long, and painful process for me. Learning and practicing getting my needs met appropriately has been equally difficult.

I went through impulse logs daily and picked up my *Bodily Harm* book written by Karen Conterio and Wendy Lader, often. Not only to refer to it, but to read what the staff and other patients wrote about me. Sometimes that is what kept me going on the road to recovery. I must say I did not make it alone and personally I believe nobody can. I had to work very hard, moment to moment, to stay injury-free. Sarah, who was with me in the program, and I phoned daily, with our daily "highs and lows", and set goals for the following day. We helped each other during the times when we thought our sorrow would swallow us. I think that is what helped me the most the first three years. It was like continuing parts of the program after we left. The hardest part upon leaving the program was to sadly end some unhealthy relationships and to set boundaries in which I was comfortable with others. Upon leaving the program, I stumbled and relapsed the first year, but it was not the same because now I knew better and had tools to stay injury-free.

These last five years could not have been successful without the love and support of a generous and extraordinary therapist, patient friends, and my spirituality. It took risks, trust, and faith to make it along with all I learned in the S.A.F.E. Alternatives program. Self-Injury is a choice and one I can certainly live without. I still keep a folder of impulse logs close by; however my impulses have become farther and farther apart and the folder sometimes appears dusty. The biggest victory was learning how to express my anger appropriately, which I denied for 20 years. It took a lot of practice, but today I can finally say that I know how to appropriately express all emotions. The biggest challenge I face today is dealing with uncomfortable feelings and feelings of abandonment. Going through them is the only way now. I like to think of it as a change of seasons. Sometimes it rains, and rains hard. I always get up now, however, and claim victory. Just like coping with the winter storm—you shovel your way out and move on. I still have to deal with my issues and I still struggle dealing with certain family relationships in a healthy way and unfortunately some had to end.

Now, five years later, I have finally found the peace within that I was always searching for, a peace I didn't think could ever exist. I am more assertive, have better boundaries, and most of all I never want to revisit that lonely place I was in while injuring. Self-injury is simply a part of my history now and it seems like it was a hundred years ago. I will never revisit that place again because it does not exist anymore. I consider myself recovered from self-injury. It is not that I don't have issues that need to be addressed anymore, but I don't need to injure to deal with them. I entered the program believing I was a hopeless case, a lost cause. When I left, I knew this was not true. I had a new confidence in myself. In fact, someone important in my journey of healing wrote in my book as I left the program, "I think you finally got it". Today, I know I did. It isn't perfect, life is still bumpy, but I am much safer, happier, and content than I ever have been in my life. My heartfelt thanks to you S.A.F.E. Alternatives!

Judy Redheffer

It is commonplace of modern technology that problems have solutions before there is knowledge of how they are to be solved.
—John Kenneth Galbraith

How I Got Here

I've started this story a million times in my head. I've put off writing it because I don't know how to start it, end it, and I don't know what message I want to send to you, the reader. It all seems very odd when you consider that the "story" in question is not some piece of insightful fiction or well-researched study, but simply and plainly, a brief autobiography. A recounting of what happened to me over a few select years. But this task, of telling my story, seems almost impossible whenever I try to complete it. It's almost like I don't really know what happened. How did my life happen like this? How did I get here?

So in an attempt to make the telling of my story easier, I have dug out all of my old papers. I figure this will be easier than staring at a blank piece of paper and expecting the right words to somehow come to me, wishing I could remember that perfect sentence I constructed in the shower two days ago.

So I sit here surrounded by the artifacts of my journey. There is an old briefcase full of college items—midterm failure notices, withdrawal forms, and unfinished class assignments. There are countless cards and letters, most of the "We haven't heard from you, are you OK?" variety. Mixed in with the papers are photographs. I am surprised to realize that none of them are of me. Instead, they are pictures others sent to me while I was in hospitals—maybe to show me what I was missing. There are folders for all of my hospital stays, and I even find one of the orange plastic admission bracelets I once had to wear. Of course, there is the thick white binder I filled during my stay at S.A.F.E.. That's the real gem, the meat and potatoes of this jumble of random notes and papers. The real work of my journey is represented inside this binder. Not just the 16 written assignments I had to complete like every other S.A.F.E. patient, but stacks of impulse control logs, my paintings, poems, and little seemingly mundane things like a copy of the daily schedule that make me remember the details of my life a little better.

These papers are hard to look at. Looking at a history assignment I never finished because I went to the hospital instead, or a photograph of smiling twenty-somethings at a party I never made it to, I feel a markedly uncomfortable combination of feelings. My first instinct is to say I feel embarrassed, regretful, and ashamed, but I know to look past these thoughts to the feelings that underscore them: sadness, grief, emptiness, and perhaps a little fear as well.

How did I end up here? I find myself ruminating on this question all the time. Surely this can't be my life. My life is the one with the early college graduation, the dozens of promising job opportunities, and the happy young family living in a clean and green neighborhood with other smiling and content people *just like me*. While it's true I might not have had a perfectly clear concept of exactly how I was going to achieve all of this, I knew for sure the things that weren't going to be a part of the plan: first, the doctors and hospitals of any kind (especially those dealing with mental health), second, unhappy feelings—only those feelings that would cause a person to smile or sigh with contentment were allowed in my ideal future, and third, weird and scary things like self-injury. I have not met these life standards. I have seen more doctors than I can count, I cry frequently, and I have made a troublesome acquaintance with self-injury.

When I was 12 years old, my big brother's best friend began doing strange and frightening things to himself. As soon as my parents realized I was being exposed to such unnatural behavior, they shielded me entirely from it. I was left without any real explanation or discussion of the matter. I quickly internalized the whole ordeal, deciding I really couldn't have seen what I thought I saw. After all, who would do such a thing?

I made it through high school and finally reached what I expected to be the pinnacle of my existence: college. But all was not well for me at college. I couldn't concentrate, eat, or sleep. In fact, I could barely think straight. Anxiety and sadness seemed to fill my entire mind. Something needed to be done. Even in my addled state I knew this couldn't be right.

So my mind came up with its own relief. Or maybe it just finally remembered what it had seen five years before. I truly don't know. But the important thing was I had a solution. If I could just hurt myself and inflict a little pain, I could regain some measure of control. The anxiety became a little less fierce, the sadness a little more bearable. I was in charge, not my feelings. This newfound solution did not come without its drawbacks though. The scars, the isolation, the disassociation, people were bound to notice.

My first intervention came at a time when I couldn't go more than a few hours without hurting myself. I had managed to keep my parents in the dark, and I was just barely keeping up at school. My friends, though, figured out what I was so keen on hiding from them. They took me to the local hospital with the understanding that I would stay "just for the weekend to straighten out my sleep schedule." I was there for almost four weeks.

I can't say that I was unmotivated to get better at that hospital. I wanted to stop hurting myself. I knew it wasn't healthy, it was keeping me from reaching my goals. But I didn't get better, I didn't stop. My imagination worked out ways to continue self-injuring even while being constantly monitored by hospital staff. I dropped far enough behind in school to consider catching up impossibility. My world got smaller, shrinking to the size of a hospital ward, even while my parents, a half-continent away, learned of my situation and tried to help me get well enough to come home.

I came to S.A.F.E. Alternatives with a sincere desire to get better, but with little hope that this could actually happen. I had met very few people whom self-injured, and I considered myself a freak, someone with a fundamental flaw who could never be normal. The S.A.F.E. program opened my eyes. Suddenly, there were a dozen other people who weren't completely baffled or repulsed by me. We shared a common understanding of the power of impulses, and the equally powerful need for control. Many of us even shared remarkably similar personal histories.

I whole-heartedly threw myself into the work of S.A.F.E., filling my big binder one assignment at a time. I learned or re-learned how to manage my thoughts and feelings. Often feeling like the pre-schoolers I have taught—"What does it feel like to be sad?", or "When are you proud of yourself?" It was basic stuff, but it was what I needed at the time.

I realized how long it had been since I had cried. I couldn't cry until I believed that feeling sad wouldn't destroy me. I realized how angry I was at the people who had hurt me. I remember asking someone "What are you supposed to do when you're angry?" I knew I shouldn't hurt myself, but what was there to put in place of that? I learned about coping mechanisms. Painting, writing, talking, reading, and walking all became options for me. Even if I didn't do any of these things, I became able to have an uncomfortable feeling or impulse and let it pass without acting on it.

When I left S.A.F.E., I was full of faith in my future. I had plans to go back to school, and I was confident that self-injury would play no part in the rest of my life. I had the highest of expectations for myself. So, I promptly failed out of school and landed once more in the hospital for acting on my impulses to hurt myself. Although, reading this, it may sound as if I fell desperately short of my goals; I consider the time period to be a small setback.

Of course, at the time I considered myself a complete failure. I thought if I couldn't succeed, even after S.A.F.E., I must be lazy and unworthy. My disappointment in myself lifted as I slowly came to realize that I had just had a relapse,

I was not back at the dreaded square one. I worked very hard after that, doing all of the things I learned at S.A.F.E., and I eventually set myself right once more.

I am proud of myself for working through my relapse, but I still deal with unhealthy impulses almost every day. I would like to say I will never hurt myself again, but I believe relapse is a part of recovery. I don't think relapsing takes anything away from what I have accomplished, and looking around at the mess of papers that surrounds me, I have accomplished a lot. I am back in school and I haven't self-injured in over a year. Now I have tests with A's on them, and pictures of a smiling me, to put alongside all of these folders.

My S.A.F.E. binder will remain at the ready. While I don't like to think of a time when I will have to turn to it again for help, I know I have already done much of the work that enables me to live the life I want, complete with happiness and sadness, pride and anger, good times and bad.

Cora B.

From small beginnings comes great things.
—Proverb

As I sit to write I find myself truly amazed at the survival skills that I have developed over the years. I look back at the past 34 years and say to myself, "How did you do it?" My story is not all that unusual or unique, but it is one that has been overwhelming to me and taken me to places that no human should ever have to go. I began to injure as a child when my step-uncle was sexually abusing me. Later in life I returned to that method of survival when the pain was too great to bear. I remember the injuring be very present in my life at very specific times. Early on in the abuse the end of the abuse, disclosing to my family, and then most recently when I lost two very precious people in my life to horrible deaths and ended a relationship that reenacted the abuse I suffered as a child.

My world felt disastrous and I returned to the coping mechanism I thought brought me a sense of control. I injured on a daily basis, often several times per day. I began to look for "opportunities" to injure. I injured at home, on the way to work, at work, on the way to my therapist office, and in the parking lot at the counseling center. I did it everywhere. No one knew for a long time, but it finally became something I couldn't hide anymore. I had made all the excuses to my family and friends that I could possible make, but the lies were no longer working. I spent endless therapy sessions trying to convince my therapist that I couldn't go on, I couldn't face another day. I never allowed the relationship to become one in which I could grow and learn. I tried to avoid the emotional pain and the hole inside of me grew bigger and bigger. The pain was unbearable. I believed the injury was the only thing that took the emotional pain away. I craved the injury and I desired the façade of release. Then the day came when I knew beyond a doubt that I had two options—get help or die. There was no middle, no bargaining, I was dangerous to myself and was at risk of dying.

I trusted my therapist, my friend Cindy, and my mom to get me to safety. I couldn't do it by myself any longer. We all did some research and found S.A.F.E. Alternatives. I knew that it was a resource for help, but I never imagined it to be the life-changing event that it was. The battle was still long as it was quite the challenge to obtain an interview for admission, to get to Chicago and then make the commitment to stay. I spent three weeks prior to admission in constant company of another human being to ensure I continued to live.

I arrived on July 6, 2004, I wasn't sure where the day would end, but I knew where it had to begin. I had to see Oralee, my therapist. I had to hear one more time, "Cheri you can do this". I needed to know that someone believed in me and was willing to stick by me no matter how bad I felt. She did just that. With a hug, a quilt, and a tender smile she sent me on my way believing I would return. What no one knew is that I thought I would never return. Never return to my cats, my home, my family, and my friends, or my therapist. I didn't believe I could live through any more pain and anguish. The day ended in a hotel room in Naperville, Illinois with my mom, my niece, and Stephanie by my side.

That evening I begged my mom not to take me to S.A.F.E. Alternatives. I begged to just return home. She continued to say, "Hon, we just can't do that, you need some help." She was right, I needed some help, but I again professed my inability to do it. That was the last day I injured, the last time I abused myself.

On July 7, 2004, I signed the most important piece of paper that will ever be a part of my life. On admission I signed a "No Harm Contract". I agreed to not injure myself for 30 days. I thought to myself that I couldn't not harm for 30 minutes how would I possibly not harm for 30 days. But I agreed, thinking I would just fail again. I said goodbye to mom and Stephanie and sank into a very frightening and lonely place.

I was alone with strangers who were "going to help me". I didn't believe it, and didn't imagine it could be done. The first hours there were gut wrenching. I wanted to run back out the front door, but there was no escape. The doors were locked, but I was reminded that I volunteered to be there. The lock doors meant nothing, because if I wanted to leave I just had to sign myself out. The thought crossed my mind more than once the next 30 days, but I didn't leave and more importantly I didn't injure.

The days were long, the nights were short and restless, and the pain intense. There were days that I thought I couldn't feel another ounce of emotional pain but more came. With each release of pain came strength, strength to face one more hour, strength to choose not to injure. For the first time in my life I felt the sadness and loss of my childhood. I grieved for the little girl who lost so many things—her spirit, her will, her body, and her soul. I felt as if the step-uncle had stolen all of it, but it was his no more.

Within the first week I began to feel a spark of hope. Maybe I could live, maybe I could stop the cycle, and maybe I didn't have to injure. Then I would crash, the pain overwhelming. But I found something at S.A.F.E. Alternatives that I had never found before, something that had been with me for as long as I had been injuring. My eyes begin to see the world in a different way I began to see me. I didn't see the "me" that was the failure or the "me" that deserved the abuse. I began to see me as the strong adult woman who could take her life back. Day by day, sometimes hour by hour, and minute-by-minute I opened my eyes and saw possibilities. I embraced the little girl who was so frightened and afraid, I comforted the adult who grieved the losses, but most importantly I stopped abusing the woman I am.

Those 30 days began a journey that I had never been allowed to think about, a journey of possibilities. I get to be who ever I want to be, I get to love whoever I want to love, and I get to do whatever I want to do. He no longer holds the power; he no longer has my spirit, my soul, or my will. I began reclaiming my body one square inch at a time.

I met a lot of great friends and wonderfully supportive staff at S.A.F.E. Alternatives, but the greatest person I met at the program was me. I introduced myself to me. Did I know all of me by the end of the thirty days? Absolutely not, but I knew that I was good enough to have a relationship with me—I could love myself, protect myself, and I could risk living. I could visualize a world without injury—I was living each day without injury.

The 30 days at S.A.F.E. quickly came to an end. We all know that 30 days is really not that long. It was time to say good-bye to safety, security, and 24-hour support. It was time to fly. My journey there ended as it began. My mom and Stephanie picked me up to return to the world to continue a journey that I had only just begun.

My return to the world was with challenges and has now become exciting. I have been able to return to my job. I have developed a relationship with Oralee that is very therapeutic where I learn and grow with each encounter. I have a huge support system because I have chosen to let people in and I have chosen to live. As I write this, I am embarking on a Masters degree and a future that I get to decide. For me the greatest decision was deciding not to injure. I did not realize that when I signed the "No Harm Contract" that I signed it for life, but that is what I am choosing. It has now been four months of no injury. I think about injuring every day, but every day I choose to stop the abuse. I choose to live.

Cheri

The highest possible stage in moral culture is when we recognize that we ought to control our thoughts.
—Charles Darwin

Hi my name is Laura D and I have recovered from self-injury. I started injuring as a child, around the age of seven. I remember my first time like it was yesterday. My dad just came back from Vietnam and we had moved back on base in Michigan. I was in second grade. From that very first time I found something that helped me cope with being a child. The injuring got real bad when I was in fourth grade and up. I learned many ways of doing things and just turned out to be the family klutz. Nobody caught on to what I was doing except that I was accident-prone. How at that age I thought of some of the things I did I'll never know, but I do know it worked, for a short period of time.

I didn't have a happy childhood. We moved to a small town and I was now in civilian schools. I got teased from day one. I was chubby and I had a strong accent. That didn't go over very well in a small town. Even the teacher gave me a lot of problems. I remember being yelled at the very first day of classes in my new school. There's a difference between military and civilian schools and I found that out right away. In military schools, everyone is used to moving and new kids coming in all the time. In civilian schools they don't seem to like change very much. I got teased so much; it makes me sad to even think about it. I'm glad that part of my life is over with that's for sure.

In high school my family moved again. I didn't want to move again, but had no choice. I had to go with my family. I once again didn't fit in. This school was full of cliques. I hated this town. I made my place out in the pines, which was off school grounds, where I spent all my lunch hours smoking cigarettes. At this time my injuring has increased on me and I really didn't know what to do. I didn't have any friends, except a few that would say hi to me and that's about it. I turned into someone very shy and didn't like life very much at all, but what is one to do. I was only 16 at the time. I'm still known at this time as a klutz because all my injuries at this time were to look like accidents. It was also at this time that I really started drinking and got into drugs. My life was not a pretty picture at all during this age bracket.

When I was 20, I celebrated my birthday and got raped. Two days later I tried to kill myself and I guess I could say that was the beginning of my recovery. I ended up in a psychiatric unit for six weeks. I was constantly injuring and having no clue as to why I was doing a lot of the things I was doing. I didn't know why I tried to kill myself either. I blocked it all out. My family was distraught and didn't know what to do with me honestly. All they knew is that their daughter was in trouble. My first psychiatrist told my family that I was just a spoiled brat and that's what my problem was. It wasn't until later in years that I was diagnosed with borderline personality disorder and even more years later being bipolar.

One day I was watching TV and just flipping through the channels and I turned Oprah on. There were these people on there talking my story of self-injury. I honestly didn't think anyone did what I did or to the extremes that I did, but there it was in front of me, other people that injured. I honestly was excited. I wanted to go to S.A.F.E. Alternatives, but my insurance wouldn't cover it. I wrote to S.A.F.E. and called constantly and one day I got a call stating they now accepted my insurance. So down to Chicago I went when I was 26. I stayed there for one month. I thought that they cracked me and cracked me well, but they only touched the surface of my issues. I went a period of time without injuring, but started again. A year later, I was once again accepted at S.A.F.E. Alternatives. I once again stayed injury free for only a short period of time. See, I didn't open all the way up. I didn't work hard enough even though it felt like it. Unfortunately, one month just wasn't long enough for me. I had been in counseling for seven years by now, and they didn't even know me. Hell, I didn't even know me. However, one day turned into another without injuring and today I have gone about eight years with only two minor injuries.

When I was 37, I went back to S.A.F.E. Alternatives to do some more hard work. I was struggling with not injuring so I decided to check myself in. I worked my butt off there. It was so different from the first two times I was there. I wasn't this "tough" person any longer. My shell was broken over the years and I got a lot out of treatment. I learned more of who I was. I had a great counselor and the groups, as tough as they were, were actually wonderful. I looked forward to going to them because I knew I was growing.

I also sought treatment for my drugs and alcohol addiction, which helped me when I was at S.A.F.E.. I no longer ran from myself. I learned to face my fear. I live by the motto "No Fear, Face Everything and Recover". I also live by the motto that "Secrets Kill." Having those two mottos stuck in my head helped me a great deal to just open up no matter what the cost would be. I couldn't get into any trouble. I was no longer a kid.

What S.A.F.E. did for me was to help me find myself to find a new life. I know that injuring is not an addiction, but one thing that really helped me out was working the 12 steps of alcoholics anonymous, which I am involved in. I learned that my life was unmanageable while injuring and I didn't like that. Then I learned that a power greater than myself could restore me to sanity, and I made a decision to turn my will and my life over to the care of God. This might not work for some, but it helped me a great deal. I also did many impulse logs, which I learned how to do from S.A.F.E.. The impulse log, along with all the assignments can be found in the book *Bodily Harm*.

Today I am ever so grateful to S.A.F.E. Alternatives. They helped me save my life. They didn't do it for me, I did that. But what they did do is help guide me and help me learn that there is a way to end the injuring. I didn't think I'd ever make it honestly, but now I have the eight years in, which seems like a miracle.

One thing that I'd like to say is don't give up. There is hope out there even if you can't get into treatment. They took just about everything from treatment and put it in their book *Bodily Harm*. That book is like my second bible. I read it a lot and do the exercises that are included, along with doing an impulse log. I find that today I don't obsess about injuring. It's a rare occasion that I even think about it, but when I do, I sit down and write out an impulse log which helps me figure out what I am feeling, anything that may have happened, and that I have other alternatives to injuring. I feel like I have been born again, but this time I have chosen the life I want instead of being instructed by parents. My life is a lot different today. I have choices, which I didn't think that I had when I was younger. Sure I still have some difficult times, but I try to not let them run me. I know that today my life is completely different. I have started back in college, I have a job, I have my own place, and I have two cats. All of which I didn't have before. I know that in recovery more things will come. I started a yahoo group which is called "NoFEAR-SAFE_Approved". Here there is recovery. It's about people from all walks and all stages in their lives wanting help. I apply the things that I have been taught at S.A.F.E. and they approve of everything that this group is doing. That is where the title has come from. Face everything and recover and you'll be in the beginning of your recovery to a healthier life.

Laura D.

Problems are only opportunities in work clothes.
—Henry J. Kaiser

To tell my story I have to start from the beginning, the very beginning. You see, throughout my life I have always seen myself as "that girl". As a toddler I was "that little girl" who's only friend was an imaginary snake named Sniggly. He was bright green, wore a Yankee's baseball cap, and drove a 1983 orange Ford pickup. His uncle was actually the first basemen for the Yankees. I was known to wave at him as he drove away. Not only did I have a vivid imagination, but I also had a creative side. When I was three, my parents took me house hunting and I walked into a house that had different colored carpet in each room and said that we couldn't live there because the carpets didn't match.

As I grew older I became known as "that girl" who had the perfect golf swing and as a result, I was one of the best junior golfers in my county. I also became interested in theater and the performing arts. By the time I was ten, I had starred in over ten local theater productions. Was I happy? Generally speaking, yes, but what people didn't see was that I was "that little girl" who was molested by someone very close to me and this has altered the way I think about love. They also missed the fact that playing golf became a quest for perfection that has lead to me giving up anything I would try so I wouldn't have the chance to fail.

As a teen in high school, I became "that girl" who was on the varsity boys soccer team, made cheerleading look easy, was in every theater production, was second in my class, got to live in a historic manor house, and study in England. Again, the thing my peers missed was that I had become "that girl" who was so depressed that some days I literally couldn't lift my head from my pillow. My parents forced me to try out for cheerleading to get me to socialize and would actually ground me from my house. They also missed that I had two suicide attempts under my belt by the time I graduated.

As a young adult, I became "that girl" who had fully succumbed to depression. I began to find ways to make that pain real—I began self-injuring. I believed that no one knew anything about it. I lied to myself and everyone around me. Luckily, my parents were more aware than I believed and they got me into S.A.F.E. Alternatives and my life suddenly changed. In the beginning, I was so mad that my secret was found out and that people were trying to make me give up the one thing that made me completely happy. I even tried to sabotage my stay at S.A.F.E. in the beginning. Again, lucky for me, the counselors there knew exactly how to change my mind and the thing that I thought was going to be a horrible experience actually became one of the most rewarding and positive things in my life.

I am not saying that my stay at S.A.F.E. was easy or that it was a magical pill I took that made my depression go away, but the tools and friendships learned there were instilled into me. I just had to choose to use them. Unfortunately, I chose not to use the tools immediately after leaving. Although I remained at S.A.F.E., my depression continued. This is where my story becomes unique because I ended up having Electro-Convulsive Therapy, ECT, also known as shock therapy. I can honestly say that I would not be here without it, but it came with a huge price to pay—memory loss. As a result, I can't actually remember most recent memories I have had including my stay at S.A.F.E.. For the first year after my treatments I went through a rough period because of the memories I lost and the weight I gained, but I am the happiest I have been since I can't remember when. I found Buddhism and my spirituality, which has led to my peace of mind. I still have my ups and downs, but I am now at a place where I can utilize the tools I have learned over the years and find the positives even in a down day. Because of this I am now able to concentrate on my art. I am a jewelry designer and I have just started my own collection. I am getting ready to own my own place and move out on my own for the first time. There is a poem that I recite every morning that really helps with my self-confidence. It is by Joseph Merrick a.k.a. the Elephant Man. Believing that something as beautiful as this poem can come from someone as troubled and insecure as he had to be really helps the way I think and maybe it can help you too. The first part goes like this:

> 'Tis true my form is something odd,
> But blaming me is blaming God,
> Could I create myself anew?
> I would not fail in pleasing you.

I guess you could say "that girl" who used to be so depressed and insecure is still depressed and insecure. I now know I can let myself be "that girl" who knows happiness, life, and love and I can't wait to become "that woman" who is married with kids.

MG

The following pages are filled with contributions from the S.A.F.E. Alternatives program current staff. They consist of various experiences in the Safe Alternatives program. It is a different perspective than that of an injurer. This section might be extra important to one thinking of treatment, for a loved one of an injurer, or for a parent or loved one who is or has been in treatment for self-injury before.

Hope has as many lives as a cat or a king.
—Henry Wadsworth Longfello

HI, YOU'VE REACHED S.A.F.E. ALTERNATIVES!

I have been the Admissions Coordinator for S.A.F.E. Alternatives for 3 ½ years. It is a new day. I begin by checking the messages in my voicemail. I hear so many stories: parents shocked and scared for their children, self-injurers who are desperate, helpless and hopeless, therapists looking for new ways to help their clients. One thing is clear; they are all searching for a way to stop themselves or someone they care about from injuring. It is my privilege to let them know that there is hope, self-injury is a choice, and help is available.

I interview prospective patients over the phone to obtain their history and assess their motivation. I can sense the fear and hesitation in the voices. The questions I have to ask are personal and probing. I continue to be amazed at the honesty and depth to which people are willing to go and explore issues that they would rather leave untouched. I try to be gentle and invite them to reveal the stories at their own pace. It is important to hear them speak of their motivation and their determination to fight the one thing that has given them comfort in the past. Many work long and hard to get to the program and agree to do whatever it takes. Some call in fear and trepidation because they have been threatened with something worse if they do not seek treatment. They may not want to give up self-injury. Often they come to realize that it is just that they don't know how they will give up self-injury. We can help with that.

Getting funding is one of our biggest challenges. Most insurance will work with us, but some people don't have insurance. Some people have worked long and hard to get here, only to have the funding fall apart at the last minute. This can be so disappointing. This is my biggest struggle, knowing that someone is motivated and ready to come, and then not able to do it. We review all the documents and think creatively and sometimes can work something out. If not, I try to help them with suggestions to enhance their outpatient treatment.

Once a patient enters S.A.F.E., the hard work begins. My hope is that they will open up quickly so they will receive the greatest benefit from their treatment; however, everyone works at his or her own pace. Some come in the door "running". Others need lots of support and encouragement to take the first and second step. As the days unfold, patients become comfortable and begin to tell their stories. I am fortunate to facilitate two of the regular groups. It is an honor to sit with a wounded soul and be part of their healing process. They are each so courageous and so brave to open up and disclose long held secrets. Disclosure frees them from the weight and pain of the past. They are able to look at themselves as they never have before. As they confront and change their old beliefs, they are a catalyst for change in the entire group. I admire the way they are able to call one another to be the best that they can be. Denial has no place here and is quickly challenged. Feelings are identified, felt, and shared. It isn't easy. I tell them that this is most likely the hardest work they will ever have to do. It is also the most rewarding with life-long effects.

Thirty days pass very quickly. What once seemed like "forever" is now over and done with. The majority of the people walking out the door have changed dramatically. They now look alive and want to live. You can see it in the way they move and talk. They are radiant! There are some who have only begun their journey. They have new options and are making healthier choices, and they are aware that they must make some changes in their life before they can complete their work. They may be back in a few years to finish up. If a patient breaks the safety contract and is discharged early, the door is open to return in 60 days. They leave fully aware of how their self-injury affects all around them. I often hear that they have learned as much from this experience as if they had completed the 30 days.

I am constantly learning from our patients and I have been changed tremendously by this work. It is a joy to see a person blossom and come to believe in themselves. It is a gift to work with them for 30 days and be able to observe the changes. It makes my day to get that call or e-mail that says, "I'm one year injury free," "I'm three years injury free," "I've just graduated magna cum laude," "I'm giving talks to emergency room doctors about how to deal with self-injury." My hope is that some day help will be more widely available to all self-injurers. There are so many who are desperately in need.

Joni Nowicki, Admission Coordinator
1-800-DONTCUT

Our greatest foes, and whom we must chiefly combat, are within.
—Miguel de Cervantes

This book is filled with the stories of courageous people determined to enjoy life free of self-injurious behavior. They are living examples of S.A.F.E.s acronym, "Self Abuse Finally Ends."

We developed the S.A.F.E. Alternatives program almost 20 years ago with the belief that choosing self-injury as a coping strategy will inevitably drain people of their identities, productivity, and happiness. Rather than collude with our clients perceived weaknesses, we focus on helping them to embrace their strengths. We believe that no matter what they may have been through in life, identifying and facing their issues is a healthier choice than buffering feelings with self-injurious behaviors.

Our hearts have been touched by so many people who against all odds, worked hard to persevere and commit to allowing themselves to tolerate intensely uncomfortable feelings and challenge ensuing irrational thoughts rather than turn to the temporary quick fix of self-injury.

Judy and Sarah are two such remarkable women who are testaments to the resiliency of the human spirit. Their goal is simple; to empower individuals to make healthier choices by sharing what has worked for others.

Karen Conterio & Wendy Lader

S.A.F.E. Alternatives
1-800-DONTCUT
www.selfinjury.com

Hope is the feeling you have that the feeling you have isn't permanent.
—Jean Kerr

My name is Cindy Miller and I started my career here at S.A.F.E. Alternatives three years ago as a registered nurse. I have since had the opportunity to do an internship with the program as part of my M.S.W. training, and currently work as both a registered nurse and licensed social worker. My experience in doing both has helped me to better experience what a patient coming S.A.F.E. Alternatives experiences because I have had the opportunity to be involved in all aspects of their care; following them from admission to discharge.

As the nurse, I am involved in many aspects of a patient's care. There are the obvious duties such as medication dispensation and education, and monitoring medical conditions, to the less traditional nursing roles such as facilitating groups and milieu management. I think that it is important for the nurse, the case managers, and the various treatment team members to know what the patient is experiencing in all aspects of programming at any given time. One of the ways we at S.A.F.E. accomplish this is to have the interdisciplinary team meet on a routine basis to discuss patient progress in programming through staffing and processing after each group. Our team communicates so closely that we often hear patients initially express frustration that "Everybody on the team knows everything". Later in programming, patients are able to see the benefit of having the entire treatment team versed on their issues.

One of the things that attracted me to the S.A.F.E. program is the unique philosophy. I can see the benefit of having a strength-based program, where the motivation to get better rests with the patient. Patients have to acknowledge that self-injury is a choice, and they have to be motivated to make other choices in dealing with stress. We do not remove all the items from the milieu that a person can injure with, and we do not do things to avoid a patient experiencing impulses. While patients are here, we want them to experience what they are feeling when they are at home, whether that is anxiety or anger We teach them to tolerate these feelings, and to express them in a healthy manner. Teaching patients to tolerate their feelings without resorting to destructive behavior leads to self-determination and empowers them to take control of their life.

The growth that a patient experiences when they learn to be proficient in mastering their life and illness is one of the things which provide meaning in my work. The individuals that come to our program have been experiencing distress in various areas of their lives: psychological, social, and emotional. In part, because of their experiences and because they have received inconsistent treatment-which further exacerbates their feelings of inadequacy and failure, these patients come to us with a self-loathing. At times patients cannot even look us in the eyes for the fear of rejection they might find there. To be part of a team that helps to facilitate a shift in individuals from feeling they are both worthless and hopeless, to an individual who has value and options in life, is extremely gratifying.

In the years that I have worked at S.A.F.E. Alternatives, I have seen this phenomenon numerous times. I purposely use the term phenomenon because what transpires is grander than the ordinary. I would like to share one example with you. A few years back we admitted a woman in her early forties, who had suffered from emotional, physical, and sexual abuse. Her self-concept was so low that we spent the first week of her treatment challenging her to maintain eye contact with the staff. Throughout her 30 day stay she struggled to take risks, and meet the challenges that the treatment team laid before her; all the while, working to gain acceptance of herself; trusting that she was worthy of the care and concern of others. I happened to be the nurse on duty on her 30th day; the night she was to be discharged. What I witnessed with this patient that evening has left a lasting impression on me, both personally and professionally. You see, not only did this patient learn to maintain eye contact, and improve other social skills; she got up before the staff and her peers, and with karaoke in hand, sang "Wild Thing". This nurse, whose heart was swelling with pride and optimism for this patient's future, silently wept behind the desk. For me, this story exemplifies the miracles we witness, and the work we are fortunate enough to perform at S.A.F.E. Alternatives.

Nothing in life is to be feared. It is only to be understood.
—Marie Curie

I had the opportunity to work in the S.A.F.E. program one day as a counselor who was "floated" from my regular unit to the S.A.F.E. unit for training. As I attended the first group of the day, I had an overwhelming sense that this was a program where patients were working hard and were highly invested in recovery from self-injury. When I heard of an open position in the program, I applied and joined the treatment team. The first role-play group that I attended was a defining moment for me as a staff member. A female patient was confronting her ethnicity and those who teased her throughout life. She was shaking and looked fearful and hesitant to begin. Her voice was initially soft and timid, but as she continued to speak through the tears and almost palpable pain, her voice became louder and firmer. As the group helped her affirm herself, she was transformed before our eyes. When asked if she believed the truth of her worth as a human being, she said, "Yes, I will believe this now." That moment will forever define for me the hope of this program and the privilege it is to be a part of the S.A.F.E. Alternatives treatment team.

Laura Rollins

Don't compromise yourself. You are all you've got.
—Janis Joplin

The most exciting experience for me is when our clients would come in very depressed, anxious, scared, and in fear of what will happen to them without their friend, "self-injury".

As our clients explored and explored their surrounding issues in group settings, and got more in touch with their feelings, they would have these "Ah Ha" moments that were just brilliant. They were able to see that they could get in touch with their feelings and; moreover, are able to get their power back from their parents, abusers, friends, and so forth.

Through simply talking and feeling, our clients were able to see more clearly, they would appear to be more hopeful. Various weeks would get tougher and tougher for our clients because of suppressed emotions surfacing up. Every time this would happen, I would congratulate them for giving them permission to feel their emotions without resorting to self-injury.

It's all about empowerment, being more vocal, and exploring the underlying feelings of anger. This would be more apparent when our clients would get to assignment number 13, "Saying good-bye to self-injury." Many of our clients would write letters to their self-injury and state, "Good-bye, self-injury, I will miss the relief you gave to me, but you were really never my friend, you were my enemy and I hate you."

Jaslyn Singh, Behavioral Health Associate, M.S. (Safe Alternatives)

The motto should be: Forgive one another; rather, understand one another.
—Emma Goldman

Welcome to the S.A.F.E. Alternatives program. We are so glad that you are here. I have been working with the S.A.F.E. program since 2001. When I first started, I worked just three days a week as a therapist. Shortly after that I became the program coordinator and am now the program manager, working full-time. I miss working with the patients in individual, family, and group therapy; however, know that my skills and expertise are serving more patients and families in my current role.

I wear many different hats as the program manager. My responsibilities include clinical supervision of the S.A.F.E. Alternatives treatment team, recruiting highly qualified staff, daily operation of the program, program and staff development, representation of the S.A.F.E. program within the hospital and community, marketing, fiscal management, and patient/family/professional/community education about self-injury. The most important task I have is ensuring that the mission of the S.A.F.E. Alternatives program occurs every day, every group, and with every patient. You may not get an opportunity to get to know me; however, I will have the privilege to know each and every one of you as I guide the treatment team in identifying your individualized treatment plan. My office opens up into the dayroom, and my door is always open to you.

I want to thank you for coming to the S.A.F.E. program. My heart goes out to you on your first day; you may be very scared. My heart will sing with yours on day 30. The transformation is amazing, you should be so proud! If it were not for brave individuals such as you, willing to take the challenge and make the choice, the S.A.F.E. Alternatives program would not exist.

Michelle M. Seliner, MSW, LCSW
Program Manager
S.A.F.E. Alternatives
(630) 305-5011
mseliner@edward.org

I am always with myself, and it is I who am my tormentor.
—Leo Tolstoy

Recovery
By Lisa Marie Brodsky

I settle back into the beige, high-backed chair and listen to the other women speak. Dragons escape through their mouths, freeing, coaxing these women toward the light.

It's when the worms crawl out of the hole that I'm finally able to breathe. It's when I can't hide in room 15, must be social. I sit in a chair across from another woman in a

chair and yell at her like she is my father. Her creamy, smooth face starts to grow stubble, smokes a cigarette in front of my face. I stare at her through the smoke and end it.

Outside in the real world, I move and the world flies by in baby carriages and halos of patchouli smoke. I squirm down the road. I will not be stepped on. The road will not

blister with heat. I will not burn and disintegrate into the dry Illinois air. I step into the crowd and look people in the eye, cloud to cloud. I easily breeze through my kitchen, my

bathroom where little hells stacked up against me. I blow the dust away. I say no to that extra cup of coffee. I'm moving down the road looking around, the corners not hidden;

big, black ridged tires do not track me down. I am no one's road kill. I am no one's embarrassment, no one's guilty look. I am the book they close with a sigh.

Lying to ourselves is more deeply ingrained than lying to others.
—Fyodor Dostoyevsky

Christy

Imagine being locked in a prison for a crime you did not commit and having no way out. This explains the majority of my life except my prison was an emotional one and it would not be until years later that I would find my way out. I self-injured in various forms from ages 5–21. I do not remember exactly why I began injuring, nor do I remember anything about the first time I did it. All I remember is how it made me feel. I felt in control all of a sudden. Nothing else in the world mattered anymore.

From a young age I felt different. I was always made fun of at school and did not have any real friends, although at times I thought I did, but I would always end up being hurt. I never thought anyone understood me. I felt as though I did not belong in this world because I felt so different from everyone else. In elementary school, I remember practically begging teachers to let me do work for them during recess so I would not have to stand by myself. When I began high school, I thought things would be different and they were for a while, but then it turned out that I was really all alone again. Most people say they will never forget their high school years because for most it was a time of learning, growing, forming friendships, and preparing for the future. I will never forget high school because for me it was a time of suicide attempts, hospitalizations, and acting on self-injury. By my junior year, my high school found out about the self-injury and tried to intervene, but eventually I was asked to leave. At this point, I thought my life was over. Still, I continued to injure because I knew of no other way to deal with my feelings.

During this time, a man my father worked with was watching 20/20 one night and heard about a place called S.A.F.E. Alternatives. My parents and I looked into the program and my parents made arrangements for me to go. However, the night before I was scheduled to fly out to Chicago, we received a call from my insurance company refusing to pay for me to attend S.A.F.E.. There was no way my family could afford to pay so I was unable to go. Again, I thought my life was over. I thought this was my last hope and I did not know what I was going to do. It would not be until four years later that I would realize that this was apart of God's plan for me and that I was simply not ready to give up injuring yet.

I went on to college but the self-injury followed me. I injured everywhere and could turn anything into a tool to injure with. While in college, I went through periods where I could stop for a short time or only injure every now and then, but I was never able to really stop.

In the fall of 2002, I went downhill fast. This time I realized how much I was hurting the people who cared about me and realized that I needed help. I lost the respect of most of my family and friends and I was slowly killing myself. After having forgotten about the S.A.F.E. program for years, I suddenly remembered the 1800-DONTCUT number and called. This time I made all of the arrangements myself and on December 18, 2002, I was on a plane to Chicago. I do not remember too much about that flight except I was a nervous wreck. I think the worst part was that I did not know until I arrived whether my insurance company would pay this time. However, everything worked out and I was admitted into the program.

S.A.F.E. is like no other hospital I had been in. The patients are treated as productive members of society. The therapy is very intense. A few days into my stay I was ready to leave because I did not think I was capable of completing the program and remaining injury-free. However, my peers talked me into staying and for that I am grateful. We were required to do two role-plays and on the day before I left I did a role-play where I said goodbye to self-injury. I felt empowered and confident that I would be ok. S.A.F.E. Alternatives saved my life and gave me a new life. The program gave me the key I needed to get out of the emotional prison I was in.

After leaving S.A.F.E. I had one slip. It was the worst feeling in the world. It just was not the same now that I had learned that there is another way to live. I have not found the need to injure since March 3, 2003. That is not to say that it has been easy and that I do not still struggle. It does get better though. Each day gets a little easier. I still use the tools I learned at S.A.F.E. and I have alternatives I use when I am struggling. I also remain in therapy where I continue to practice everything I learned while in S.A.F.E.. For my stay at S.A.F.E. was only the beginning of my recovery process. The work had only begun. S.A.F.E. helped me to take an in depth look into myself and focus on the feelings behind the self-injury. I am gaining the respect back from my family and I have great friends who have supported me along the way. I also have contact with other recovering self-injurers. I am currently going to school to be a social worker so I can help others find hope. I have a lot of work to do still, but I believe that with out self-injury in my life I can achieve anything I want.

Christy T.

I have striven not to laugh at human actions, not to weep at them, nor to hate them, but to understand them.
—Benedict Spinoza

Alice Looks into the Mirror in S.A.F.E.'s Bathroom
by Lisa Marie Brodsky

Poor Alice used to lock herself up in the bathroom
and eat too many crumpets and sob and do things
that would horrify the Mad Hatter.
Gazing into the looking glass, Alice sees
a leopard stepping out of a kitten suit.
Her tightly wound braids loosen
and she hears, "*It doesn't have to be that way
anymore.*" She hears the child stop crying
with little hiccups that sound like staccato
notes. Her battle scars are fading, the fight
with the caterpillar, the twins,
the Queen. Looking into the mirror, they
were all prisms of herself, anyway.
But she sees beauty as well. She sees
a quiet expectant waiting of relief. The corners
of her mouth no longer turn downward.
She sees potential, the many journeys
she has yet to pursue: no hallucinogens,
no need for weapons or fear.
Alice opens the bathroom door, returns
to the common room. She sees time well spent

It is easy to live for others; everybody does. I call on you to live for yourselves.
—Emerson

Recovery is possible. The program does work. All the groups, all the logging, all the feeling, and all the writing assignments do have a purpose and I am proof. The story that brought me to S.A.F.E. is like many others—full of hurt and pain, numbness and anger, and so many others. But this story is not about that. This is the story of my life during the last two years, after I left S.A.F.E..

    I entered S.A.F.E. March 18, 2002. Like everyone there, I had my doubts, and asked myself "Will this work?" Will their people really understand me?, Do I really want this?" I say I do, but really, deep down is it worth it? I took hold of my fears and doubts, and made the commitment to give the program a fair shot. By this point, I really was feeling like it was the best chance I had for recovery and quite possibly my only real chance. So I did the assignments, went to each group, spoke up, and opened up. I listened to the other stories and gave feedback and received feedback. I kept a journal of how things went and what was learned that really made an impact.

    After 30 days, I graduated the program. Was it easy? No. I was used to my feelings always being put down and being hurt. I was terrified of people and of facing the past. I had to learn to express myself despite these things. It was work and it was terrifying and exhausting. Truly, I don't believe that it is truly ever easy for anyone, but I made it. I returned home to a family situation that hadn't changed really, but I had changed, and that was what mattered. When I entered the program, I was deeply depressed and injuring frequently; wonder why bother, I don't matter, no one cares anyway. But when I came out I had realized that people do care. That what my family had been telling me was wrong. I could see how messed up their behavior was. I could finally see how it affected me and brought me down, and with these realizations, came a new joy living. My first weeks, even months home were not easy. I was often triggered and I was unsure of who I was with all these changes that had occurred. It was a constant struggle to fight against the put downs my father was putting out, but day by day, I did it. I logged and I stayed close to a friend that had been with me through so much already. I have had relapses. Just because you go through S.A.F.E. doesn't mean that you are cured, but I have persevered.

    The most important tool S.A.F.E. gave me during the program itself was the writing assignments because through them I was able to access thoughts that I couldn't get to by talking. After the program, the most important tool was my alternatives, especially the one that says, "Talk to a friend." Holding things inside and letting them bounce around unchecked was the major trigger. Taking in what others were saying about me or to me, without a second thought, was a major trigger, and still is to this day. Learning that people do care what I think and feel, realizing that my friend would talk to me when I called from the program or even after I came home, that he would make time to meet with me if I asked, and learning that the people I went through this with would continue to support me when I came home. This was the single biggest assist to my staying safe.

I have relapsed four times since I have been home. Maybe to some they don't consider that success, but to me, I know it is. Before, what I was doing controlled me. It was a compulsion, and much of the time I wasn't even sure that what was setting me off each of these times was a choice, each time it was born of fear, usually fear of abandonment and here again. Learning to speak and to dare to trust, are my biggest defense. Before S.A.F.E., I stayed in my room, never went out, and even going to a movie was rare. I went out, did what I had to, and came home and straight to my room. If I went to one movie a year, it was pushing it. I didn't go camping, I rarely went to the bookstore, and I never did things with groups of other people. Being around large groups, and by large I mean more than two other people, it was a struggle before to look someone in the eye, to look up as I was walking, and to speak up and disagree with someone on something. I was also on six different medications including, Celexa, Nortriptiline, Wellbutrin, Depakote, Seraquel, and another I don't remember. Now, after leaving the program, I do make eye contract and routinely look around when walking. The movies are a frequent occurrence, and I've even been camping. Not only did I go camping, but it was a large gathering of several different groups, and in my group alone there were 50 people. Before the program, getting out of bed was a chore, something I dreaded, for it was the only place I felt safe. Now I look forward to each day with excitement and wonder. I still have those days where all I really want is to stay in bed, but they are infrequent.

Before the program, I couldn't keep a job, and I was so unfocused and depressed that I really couldn't function. Since the program, I had one job that didn't work out because I was still adjusting to being home, but the second one that I took through a temp agency has worked out beautifully. I was hired full-time and have been in my current position 21 months, six months as a temp and the rest as a permanent full-time employee. I don't dread getting out of bed for work, as I look forward to it.

I had few friends before, but now I have too many to count. I spend so little time at home these days which it's like visiting a strange country. I work full-time and spend time with my friends most nights of the week. It hasn't been easy, much has happened since I've been home, and much of it has not been good. I've gotten a job, bought a car, found a religion that fits me better than the one I was raised with, and because my father didn't approve, he threw me out of his house and hasn't spoken to me since and it has now been nearly nine months. I moved into a place with so many animals, it wasn't even sanitary, with no inner door, and that was very cold at night, as I moved in December. Amongst all this, I lost two ferrets, my grandfather, my uncle, and also attended the funeral of my friend's 18 month-old grandson. I left the first place I moved to and moved in with a friend. Due to financial reasons, I have endured all this without any of the meds I was once on. This is not to say meds are bad, they had their place in my recovery, in helping me endure the challenges. There are also some people that have conditions that need them for life, but I think many self-injurers are over medicated and urge caution against that. There is the temptation to medicate away an issue instead of truly treating and dealing with it. But I don't believe that is true recovery.

This whole journey since I left the program has been hugely challenging, and the majority of the time I stayed safe. This is success. I have found that it simply doesn't work for me anymore. It doesn't work because I value myself too much now. I know I deserve better. I know that there are many people around who will take time to listen. I see the hurt in their eyes when I have relapsed, but still they are there for me. For a while, with everything going on, the urges were coming so intensely that I thought I must surely explode. They were lasting for days, but I fought and I won. I dared to believe that I deserve better.

I now understand that what happened to me was wrong, and what my family is telling me has been lies, that I'm OK and there never was truly anything wrong with me. With that realization comes the attitude of how dare they! And I'll be damned if I will continue the violence they have inflicted on me, they won't win anymore. I deserve better!!!! There is true healing, a healing that occurred because at the program I found acceptance. I found people that truly understood what I was going through as I fought this battle. I found I'm not alone in how I've been treated and hurt. I found that, yes, what I think and feel matters, and people will listen to me. I was given the words to express the thoughts and the feelings, and thus, to be able to deal with them. I learned to deal with the anger that so often fueled my self-injury, which I had to learn to recognize the feelings under the anger, why I was angry. I learned to determine if I was feeling hurt, lonely, or misunderstood, to address this point. By doing this, I had to slow down and give thought. At this point, I could use an alternative; I could log it, talk to someone, or put on some music. By doing so, addressed the urge and allow it to pass safely.

S.A.F.E. Alternatives is an excellent program, without it I am truly sure I would not be here right now, and I surely would not have what I have now—a job, a decent car, friends, hobbies, a spark in my eye, and hope for the future. I had to give up some things along the way, a relationship with my father for one. To be true to myself, I had to leave his house, but I gained more than I lost. I gained self-respect because at this point, I'm living my life; not the one someone else wants me to live. I had to let go of the idea of my family ever being there for me emotionally and that was a challenge. I still struggle with that one. For like everyone, I wish most deeply that my family would love and accept me, but I know that this is something that they are capable of. Is journey to recovery complete just because I went to S.A.F.E. Alternatives program? No. But it was a stepping stone I needed to start on the journey. It gave me the tools and the foundation and it was up to me to apply them.

If you're reading this book, then most likely you are looking for hope, looking for recovery, and perhaps you are considering the program. I say recovery is possible. I don't know you and don't need to. I already know our stories are very similar. I say no matter what you're told, you are worthy, you are valuable, and you can make it. I don't know what the future holds, but what I do know is that whatever comes, it is my choice how I respond to it. I have the power to live my life and I deserve to do so. That is the recovery we seek, that you can seek. That you can have if you are willing to do the work.

Angela

But I do nothing upon myself, and yet I am my own executioner.
—John Donne

I have to remind myself daily that I am a worthwhile human being. I was blessed with a schizophrenic mother who was both physically and emotionally abusive. Even after recovering from self-injury, the old tapes still play in my head. It is difficult for me to feel "good enough" to do anything just live. My daily affirmations are a big part of my recovery process.

I sometimes think about what led me to S.A.F.E.. I felt very hopeless and out of control. I recognized the fact that I could not work in my profession and felt a sense of loss. I wanted and needed help but nonetheless it was hard to accept. Other person caring for me was rare at that point in my life. I didn't know how to ask for help and trust that I would receive it. Trust is still very difficult for me. I had read the book *Bodily Harm* while I was living at a halfway house following a lengthy hospitalization. It was my dream to go and actually be a part of the program. I am so grateful that I was able to do this.

Today, I easily become frustrated with my lack of a career. In the middle of my illness, I earned a Master's degree in social work. Due to my condition, I was unable to maintain a job in my field for any significant period of time. I would get so caught up in helping others that I neglected myself. My psychiatrist describes me as a "sponge that absorbs the problems of others." I finally decided to take a break from my chosen line of work. I still keep my feet wet a little with the volunteer work that I do. Someday I will return to social work when I have maintained wellness for a significant time period. Sometimes I feel that my education was a waste and then I have to remember that it is part of what created me into the being that I am today. That being is not a bad person.

I also feel blessed to have two "parents", my dad and stepmother, who genuinely care about me and my well being. As I have mentioned, growing up I did not live in a nurturing environment. I had to fend for myself with the help of an older brother. Sometimes it feels weird to be loved and cared about. I thank God on a daily basis for seeing me through the hell that I knew and leading me to where I am now.

When I started "getting better" was when I started taking one day at a time. I only had to make choices for that day. If this was to eat right, not injure, exercise, or whatever. I just had to choose for that day and that day only. Pretty soon I started stringing "good days" together to make a period of time when things were going better in my life.

One tool I used extensively was my five alternatives that S.A.F.E. talks about. I was always able to find an alternate activity that helped me remain S.A.F.E.. I also did a lot of journaling. I would begin to feel better if I put my racing and ravaging thoughts down on paper. I have also completed the 15 writing assignments several times throughout my recovery. I save them and look back, with the assistance of my therapist, to see how my answers have changed. The insight that this provides is incredible. This has added a lot to my getting better.

I also have begun to take better care of my physical health through proper diet and exercise. I find that if I am having intense feelings about something, I can exercise it out. Making healthier eating choices has also helped me mentally and physically. I have learned that my body reacts differently when I eat certain foods such as chocolate and caffeine. Throughout the process of "getting better", I have lost a fair amount of weight. This has positively impacted my self-esteem.

Spirituality is another component to my recovery. I began attending church regularly and enriching my spiritual life. I find that my mind is less troubled with worries when I can give them up to my higher power in prayer. With this connection that I have nourished, I feel less alone in this world. For the past year, I have been discerning entering a religious order. I feel the most fulfilled when I am giving of myself to others.

My service work is a huge aspect of my life in recovery. I volunteer at three different locations each week. I work with children in a hospital, at a food pantry for the underprivileged, and at the information desk in a hospital as well. Giving of myself gives me the most incredible feeling of worth. I am employed part-time in a retail position which assists me financially yet, still allows me to engage in volunteer activities.

So it is with all of these; faith, physical and emotional nourishment, and service that I have maintained ongoing recovery from self-injury for the past 14 months. I still see a therapist about once a month and my psychiatrist twice a month. I am blessed with mental health providers who are very attentive and caring.

It is from the heart that I say "thank you" to Wendy, Karen, and everyone else at S.A.F.E. for helping me find the tools I need to get better. Even after going to S.A.F.E. twice, I did not think that I could ever recover. It took me taking the tools and applying them to my life one day at a time.

The program does work and I am very proud of my 14 months. This has been a long road for me. I was at S.A.F.E. for a few days then went back that spring and stayed for a month. I did not get better right away. Obviously with the elapsed time I stayed sick for a long time. I went from job to job and hospital to hospital then something clicked and I took things one day at a time like I talked about. I had a physician assistant last January in the emergency room bet me that I couldn't stop. It was with this challenge that I decided to make a change. He told me to come see him in a year. I really didn't know if I could do it, but I have, adding day to day to string together 14 months.

My pride of this accomplishment mounts each day that I go without injuring. My psychiatrist, on the same day, fired me but changed his mind if I would quit injuring. It was with these two incidents that I was able to change my mind and behaviors for good. I was able to show them that I could succeed at this thing called "life" and I have soared with success. Each day is a blessing now where it used to be a struggle. I am so thankful for everyone who has played a part in my recovery along the way.

Libby

Some of the reasons I am the way I am is precisely because of a negative history. Why would I erase that? If I was a black man, wouldn't I want to have the history of what that has meant? Not that you have to act on it every day it's so much a part of your decision making.
—Jodie Foster

A Stay at S.A.F.E. Alternatives
Current patient Feb, 2005

    I heard about S.A.F.E. Alternatives and my husband researched it on the internet. It seemed like the only thing left to help me. He asked if I was really interested in going there for treatment. I said, "What did I have to lose?" After all, I was pretty sure our insurance would never go for it. They wouldn't even consider it. But, my husband, therapist, and doctor all agreed with me that it was worth it and we should try. Of course the insurance company denied the request and I was ready to give up. I was tired of everything. I was tired of being shifted from inpatient to outpatient and home again no better than before. My husband appealed the decision and much to my surprise they approved the appeal. Now, I realize that I had to put up or get out. No more saying I wanted to get better but believing nothing was going to change.

    Soon everything was arranged and I was packed and it was time to go. I'm ready to run. I realize that it is up to me. I can go, work, and get well or I can chicken out. Well, we went and I took myself to the hospital, Linden Oaks, via taxi and walked into the unknown.

    I was surprised at the pleasant surroundings and how friendly everyone seemed to be. Soon, I was checked in and went to the unit. I went in and instantly thought I had stepped into the twilight zone. I was in the wrong place. I didn't belong here with all of these kids. I wanted to turn around and run.

    I expressed my concerns to the staff and they reassured me that we did have things in common. I needed to give it a chance was the advice from the staff. I found we do actually have things in common, we are hurting, have the need to self-injurer and have trouble showing our feelings.

    What I have found is a safe place where you work your rear off. I've been in several treatment centers and talk the talk. There is a safe place to feel your feelings. There is a busy day with groups scheduled from 8:30 a.m. to 8:30 p.m. The schedule isn't just on paper it actually goes on everyday. All the groups meet on time, are well staffed, and are designed to address all areas of our healing. Everyone gets a chance to talk if they want and peers give feedback along with staff. You are expected to attend all groups and encouraged to use the logs to document urges to injure and for negative thinking. You are responsible for your own treatment because you and you alone can talk, share, log, and participate. It would be easy to sit in group and just exist but that's how most of us spend most of our lives.

Everyday is busy, stressful, tiring, and long. However, everyday needs to be in order to make the most of the 30 days we've been given to make our own lives better. We have to work hard everyday and make the most of all the opportunities to grow stronger. Everyday is also a rollercoaster of emotions that gives you a rough ride and it is hard to hold on. Every night so far, I've called my husband and told him to come get me. I think I want to give up and take the easy way out. However, by morning I've realized that I do want to get better, it's going to be hard work and I can do it. Then I pull the bar down on the rollercoaster and get ready for the days ride.

S.A.F.E. has something so many treatment centers I've been in don't. They have enough staff to meet the needs of the patients. Groups aren't' cancelled because of new admissions. Medication is given on time, individual sessions are available to everyone, and family sessions are considered important and held.

I've only been here nine days, but I've already made progress that I never dreamed possible. I've been able to confront peers and staff appropriately and move on. Before I would have stuffed the feelings and obsessed about the issue. It hasn't been easy but just this seeming less small step can give me the strength to take charge of my life through healthy relationships.

The autobiography and writing assignments are a key part of the program. These assignments are important part of the treatment program. Through the writing assignments you can discover many things about yourself and deal with some issues you have not recognized or come to terms with.

The calls begging to go home are fewer and farther apart. I am seeing that I can tuck my tail and run or I can stay and work through this program. It can give me the skills to lead a happier and healthier life. I just need to remember that 30 days may seem like a long time, but I must make the best of everyday to change my life.

Kathi Knight

Today's mighty oak is just yesterday's nut that held its ground.
—Anonymous

My Story probably isn't too much different than most self-injurers. I started injuring when I was 13. To this day, I do not know why I chose self-injury instead of drinking, drugs, or another destructive coping skill. Maybe it was the Teen Magazine that I read a month earlier about self-injury, and maybe not. I might never know. I don't know why it seemed to work for me. It calmed me down and helped me keep my emotions understandable for me. What I do know, is once I started, it seemed impossible to stop.

I kept my secret for a few months. I wore long sleeves and made excuses for marks on my arm. In the beginning, I could hide it, my injury wasn't severe and I was only injuring every week or so. The only person who knew I was injuring was a friend, who was very confused about it. Then, I attempted to take my life, and my secret was found out. That is when I was placed in my first hospital. I was really scared. I knew I didn't belong in a hospital. I wasn't like the rest of the kids there. I was normal; I had a normal family, and normal life. There was nothing wrong with me. I think I was in for a month or so. The hospital focused on the suicide attempt, and didn't really help me with much of anything. But, because that was the only psychiatric hospital in the area, that was our only resource at the time. I went back there four times. During that time, my injury was getting much worse. My parents would have to take me to the emergency room to get stitches and that was a terrible experience. Hospital emergency rooms are a terrible place for most self-injurers. The staff can be so rude and inconsiderate. Most believe self-injurers are just a waste of time.

After my fourth hospitalization, my treatment team and my parents felt out of resources, and felt a long term treatment center was in my best interest. It was clear I wasn't getting any better with my therapy and trips to the hospital; in fact I was just getting worse. I believe this happened because the hospital encouraged me to use alternatives like snapping a rubber band on my wrist, using red marker to fake self-injury, and other counterproductive ways to deal with my injury. When those coping skills failed, I went to self-injury, more frustrated and discouraged than ever. I started to believe I belonged in this world of mental health, and I feared I would never get better. I had already missed so much of my high school years, and now I was sent to this long term treatment center. Boy I must be crazy.

I think the first month or so in the treatment center, I cried. I could see the heart break on my family's face when the came to visit me. I was so scared and homesick. I had no idea what to think of this place, it was nothing like the hospital experience I had come from. There were only about ten kids, and it was set up like a house. But, gradually, I became more comfortable and started to open up some. A few others dealt with self-injury who were there. We talked more about how to deal with our feelings and what I called at the time, corny coping skills. Believe it or not, those corny coping skills I learned then helped me year's later recover from self-injury. The treatment center is where I believe I lay the ground work for my recovery. I don't think at that time I was ready to give up on self-injury. But I did come out of there with a better self-esteem and more mature. I graduated high school in the treatment center and also went on a pass to my high school prom with a friend. So, now I was 18 and looking for colleges and being sent home from the treatment center after being there a year and a half.

I got into a college for the fall, and I was excited, I thought for sure I was going to be alright, and hospitals were behind me—I was wrong. Self-injury came back and the worse it has ever been. I was away at school, and was going into yet another hospital. This went on for a while. I actually don't remember much of this time. It was almost like I was a different person. I was in and out of hospitals a lot, only staying in the hospital a few days. I think the reason I experience this set back was I didn't know how to use anything I learned in past therapy and put it to work for me now. I was in a total different world now, and I was lost.

My parents and I had heard a few years back about the S.A.F.E. Alternatives program. But I don't think any of us believed I was at the point that I needed something like that. But now it became clear to my family, my treatment team and me that we had to do something. S.A.F.E. was my last hope. I was so discouraged and so lost that I feared I would be like this forever. So, I went to Chicago to what I thought was the S.A.F.E. program. Somehow I ended up at the wrong hospital. S.A.F.E. use to be at a different hospital but they moved. Somehow the place I went to forgot to mention that and well, it was a big mix up. Once I realized I wasn't at S.A.F.E., I called home and I was devastated. But within days, I was at the real S.A.F.E. Alternative program. My family got a hold of S.A.F.E. and made all the arrangements and I was finally there.

This is where my S.A.F.E. story begins. I was in S.A.F.E. for 30 days. I felt a connection with the other clients there. I felt really understood. To meet so many others that had struggled with self-injury and see how it ruined their lives and to see how much everyone wanted to get better. It was enough to motivate anyone. Don't get me wrong, I was scared, really scared. But, this time being scared was a good thing. I think it jumped started me into the program. We had a lot of groups, more that any other place I had been to. We had writing assignments, and they were not easy. I logged, and logged, and logged. We were challenged constantly by staff, by each other, and by ourselves. S.A.F.E. was the hardest thing I had ever done in my life. Emotionally I was so drained at the end of the day that I didn't even need a sleeping pill to fall asleep. I gained knowledge of myself at S.A.F.E..

After S.A.F.E. I understood self-injury was a choice. Yes, on one level I knew that before, but now I understood it was my choice and believed it was my choice. When I left S.A.F.E. my case worker and my therapist came to pick me up and learn about the program. That really helped me continue what I learned at S.A.F.E. and practice it once I was home. That was a huge part of my recovery. A year or so later, I went back to S.A.F.E., I believe I just needed to go through it once more. I was struggling at the time and needed a little help so that I would not slide far back, and I didn't. I do not see going to S.A.F.E. a second time as a failure. I have always been a slow learner, and I think it was what I needed.

Now years after S.A.F.E., I see the impact S.A.F.E. has had on me. I had made wonderful friends from the program, like Judy, whose understanding and support help me so much. I am giving up my title as a mental heath patient. When my doctor/therapist who I had for five years moved, I decided that I didn't need therapy anymore. I now just keep in touch with my case worker. I am off the medication I was on for so long, and I didn't know it would feel this good to be off of them. I hope I never need to go back on them again.

I have a full-time job that I love. I think it is a huge reason that I am where I am today. The responsibility a job put on me was good. I now feel that I can do something better than being a mental health patient and it is my work. I had quit college before, but now I am going to school at night. I like it a lot. I never thought that I could balance so much, but now I can, and I am proud of myself.

I am not cured, I am better, and I am in recovery. I still have relapses, but they are different now. I know I do not need self-injury. I know I can stop and think about what I am feeling and why I might be feeling that way, before I couldn't do that. I actually think relapses help my recovery. I learn a lot for them, and now my relapses are few and far between. My identity isn't Sarah the mental patient, it is now just Sarah.

I wanted to help others who were still struggling with self-injury. When I was talking to Judy one day on the phone, we came up with the idea for this book. See, I think I have every book on self-injury, but only a few helped inspire me. The others just triggered me into wanting to self-injure. We wanted a book that would really touch the lives of people who self-injure, and injurers that are in recovery that needed a little more support. Self-injury is such a taboo subject. I will see it on TV once and awhile, but hardly do I feel it is given an accurate portrayal.

S.A.F.E. Alternatives is not a miracle program. You get out of it only as much as you put into it. For me, it was the final chapter in my mental health life. I may never be fully recovered, but I am so much better and a lot happier than I have ever been. I believe it can only get better from here.

Sarah Brecht

Lying to ourselves is more deeply ingrained than lying to others.
—Fyodor Dostoyevsky

Kathryn Small
Current patient, S.A.F.E. Alternatives®
February, 2005

Untitled

I'm gonna get better
I'm gonna get well
I'll no longer feel
like I'm living in Hell

I won't want to hurt
I won't want to cry
in a few weeks
I won't want to die

I'm learning to do it
I'm learning to live
I'm starting to see

I'll go home after S.A.F.E.
and everyone will see
this road I am on that's leading
to a new and better me

©Kathryn Small

We hope this book has helped you. Self-injury is something that can be overcome. If you are a current self-injurer, we urge you to get help. We know recovery is possible, but we also know it is not easy. We hope this book has helped you see that there is another way. If you are a recovering self-injurer, we admire everything you have gone through to get to this point. If you are a loved one of a self-injurer, we hope this book has given you some insight to self-injury. If you are a medical professional, we hope you can see that self-injury is nothing to be afraid of and that what would be most helpful to a self-injurer is to respect them, not belittle them.

Thank you, Judy Redheffer and Sarah Brecht

If you have comments or would like to participate in a follow-up book, please contact BeyondSelfInjury@hotmail.com

978-0-595-36026-0
0-595-36026-2

Printed in the United States
59440LVS00005B/442-459